ORBIT OF CHINA

BOOKS BY HARRISON E. SALISBURY

Fiction

THE NORTHERN PALMYRA AFFAIR

Nonfiction

ORBIT OF CHINA

A NEW RUSSIA?

MOSCOW JOURNAL—THE END OF STALIN

TO MOSCOW—AND BEYOND

THE SHOOK-UP GENERATION

AMERICAN IN RUSSIA

RUSSIA ON THE WAY

ORBIT

HARRISON E. SALISBURY

OF CHINA

HARPER & ROW, PUBLISHERS

NEW YORK, EVANSTON, AND LONDON

ST. PHILIP'S COLLEGE
Not to be taken from the Library
without permission

301.2951
S1670

ORBIT OF CHINA. Copyright © 1967 by Harrison E. Salisbury. Printed in the United States of America. All rights reserved. No part of this book may be used or reproduced in any manner whatsoever without written permission except in the case of brief quotations embodied in critical articles and reviews. For information address Harper & Row, Publishers, Incorporated, 49 East 33rd Street, New York, N.Y. 10016.

LIBRARY OF CONGRESS CATALOG CARD NUMBER: 67-11331

E-R

For Charlotte

14163

Contents

Illustrations

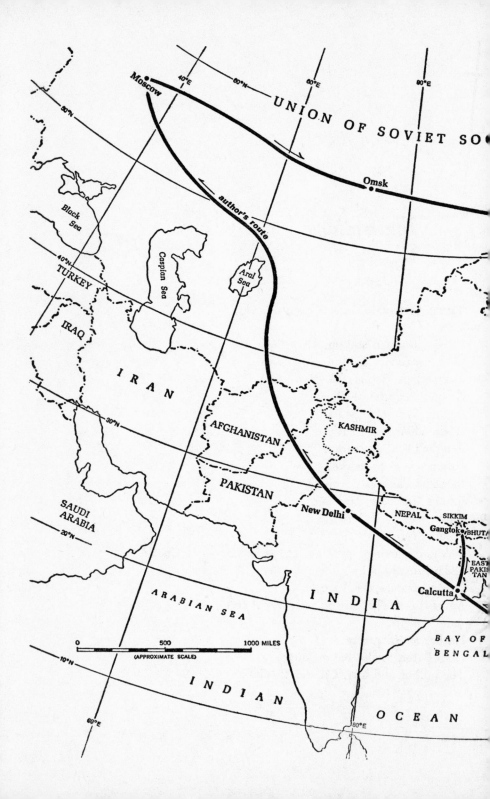

ORBIT OF CHINA

1

The Road to Lo Wu

THE ROAD TO LO WU BEGINS AT KENNEDY AIRPORT 8,657 MILES AWAY. It crosses the continent, soars over the Pacific and touches down in Honolulu, just long enough for a drive up to the quiet crater of the Punchbowl where fourteen thousand graves of World War II lie, row on row, beside a smaller field of Korean War dead. In the hot morning sunshine, the Punchbowl seemed incredibly neat, the big monument standing solid up against the shoulder of the old volcano rim and the pleasant driveway curving past the geometric rows.

A tractor was working in the western quadrant, and the raw red of new-turned Hawaiian earth was bleeding onto the green lawn.

"We're getting them in from Vietnam now," the attendant said, hitching up his chinos. "Not like Korea, of course. But they're coming in now. Almost every day. The planes bring them in."

The taxi crawled forward a hundred yards and stopped. There was Ernie Pyle's stone, convenient to the road for those who still remembered Iwo Jima—and Ernie. I remembered Ernie very clearly. Sitting on a cot at the Aletti Hotel in Algiers, the mosquito netting pushed back, his face lined and tired and thin, the bottle of whiskey, a full quart bottle of Teacher's, in his hand. He had just flown in from leave in the States, the long way, across the Atlantic to Dakar and up the coast. He was going back to the front and the GI's and he didn't like it and he wished he never had to see another front,

1

ST. PHILIP'S COLLEGE
Not to be taken from the Library
without permission

never had to write another GI story, never again had to sweat out the early-morning jump-off, the crawling forward from the lines, the lonely jeep ride into nowhere.

"Oh, God," Ernie said, "I wish I didn't have to go back to the war. I wish to Christ I never had to talk to another GI. I wish to God there never was another GI or a war or . . .

"I don't know how to say this," he went on. "But in Tunisia, the last time I was at the front I was talking to a kid. All he said, over and over again, was 'Fuck my shit. . . . Fuck my shit. . . .' Those three words. That's all. Somehow it got me."

We listened to him silently. On the boulevard outside the Aletti you could hear the rumble of trucks, a convoy or something going by.

"Oh, hell," he went on. "Don't mind me. I've had my war and now I've got to go back again and really what's there to say about it that the kid didn't say?"

He went back, of course, and if the shrapnel hadn't come his way at Ie Jima he might have been standing there in the hot sunshine smelling the faint fragrance of frangipani, following another road . . . the road to Lo Wu.

I thought of Pyle and of the war, the endless wars of our time, as the plane flew westward over the Pacific, misty and almost invisible 37,000 feet below. Ernie Pyle's war was a long time back. Then there was, or seemed to be, a simplicity about the world that no longer existed. It hadn't really been true, of course, but I thought then that I could tell the Good Guys from the Bad Guys. It seemed black and white, good and evil. I knew that Good would triumph and Evil go down to defeat.

Now there was another war and nothing was simple about it —nothing at all. There was no agreement, no easy, recognizable consensus Good, only terrible portents of Evil. The young GI's were dying again, in dirt and filth and agony, Ernie Pyle's words on their lips. Napalm was ravaging the villages, searing brown bodies along with the white, the young with the old, women and their babies, those who knew why they were dying and those who did not know a war was on.

Over the whole world there were alarm and fear lest the contagion spread, lest the engines of destruction, so much more mighty, so much more efficient (the highest kill ratio in the world, sir!), might be unloosed in ever-widening circles, fanning out from Asia and beyond.

It was this which had put me on the road to Lo Wu, set me off on a mission to the most distant ends of the earth, this time with Charlotte beside me. I was not going to the battle front. Not Vietnam. I was going beyond the fighting lines. I would by-pass the confused, sweating jungles of Indochina and try to make my way to the edge of China, climbing the high Himalayas, skirting the black deserts of Central Asia and the wilderness of Siberia, seeking the sources of the torment and the tragedy—if, indeed, they were to be found.

Was it really China that lay behind it all? Or was it, as not a few Americans believed, the United States, blundering and bludgeoning, blindly striking out in a kind of frenzy of frustration? Had China and ourselves embarked on a collision course which could lead only to world nuclear destruction? The answer was not going to be easy to get. There still was no entry for Americans into Peking. I would again knock at all the doors to China, but I had little hope that I would find one ajar. My hope was that from the long periphery it would be possible to see some things more clearly. Perhaps there were Asians whose perceptions were more keen than ours, men wiser in years of Asian life and Asian history, men who knew China better than the Chinese themselves, men who could judge better than we what was wrong and what was right in Vietnam and what was the true source of the shock waves which were proliferating around the world, setting the tractors in the Punchbowl to carving back the matted green turf and exposing the naked ocher of the volcanic clay.

China . . . was it sheer atavism which sent a chill down my spine

§ 3

as I contemplated the implications of what Peking said and Peking did? It was no longer fashionable to speak of the "yellow peril." Indeed, the very phrase seemed like an echo of an earlier naïve era, of Teddy Roosevelt, the Great White Fleet and the Boxer Rebellion. Yet what of the chauvinistic racism of China's appeals for unity of the peoples of yellow, of brown and of black color? Was this mere propaganda? I did not think so. Peril stalked the world. It swirled up in clouds from Asia—East Asia. My task was to define its shape and fix its outline.

China . . . it had taken me a lifetime to get there. Over the years I had pushed my way far to the east along Siberia's China frontier. I had peered across the Black Dragon River toward the China side. I had penetrated Mongolia as far as the Gobi and seen the Chinese and the Russians in the opening act of what was to become protracted Communist political warfare.

Now I was following the Lo Wu Road, and I wondered where it would really lead. I remembered sitting through a winter's evening with the cold rain beating down on Chicago's Quadrangle, listening to the China experts. They were all there—the brilliant young men from the State Department, the tweedy professors from London and California, the aging lady Marxists, the cheery Swedish anthropologist, the cynical old Shanghai correspondent, a Canadian businessman, an Australian lady-of-goodwill, a thick-spectacled scholar from Prague and several lively American Chinese. No one agreed on anything. I liked that.

I remembered saying, in my ignorance, that the most startling event of the twentieth century seemed to me not the emergence of the United States as the paramount power of the world. Or the spectacular rise of Russia. De Tocqueville, after all, had predicted these events a hundred years ago. No. The event of the twentieth century was China's renaissance.

China . . . what did we really know of her? And what did she know of us? Our contacts had been so fleeting and so traumatic. They went back not more than 100 or 150 years. China's culture, her language, her social heritage, her economics, her history, her religion, her philosophy, her races—all this had been and still was alien to us. As was ours to her.

China had seen, must still see, herself as the center of the world—a world whose origins were lost in antiquity, a continental island that had floated in a sea of barbarism not for centuries but for millennia.

True, for a few years we, the barbarians from the West, had ravaged her land, made slaves of her peoples, imposed crude dictates and alien ways upon her.

If we wished to understand how the past hundred years looked to China, I had suggested, we must turn to something more familiar to us—to the devastation of Rome by the Huns. We understood that. We understood that the "dark ages" put out the lamp of Western civilization for centuries until the spark of the Renaissance relighted it.

Had not the past hundred years been China's "dark ages"? And was not the lamp now being relighted in their eyes? I looked around the room in Chicago, listening to the pounding of the rain on the windows. Did one have to go to China to feel the pride of the Chinese in the re-emergence of a strong China? Did one have to go outside that room? Could it not be felt in the most casual conversation with even the bitterest of enemies of the Chinese Communists—the Chinese Nationalists?

Would I find this true in the Orient? Perhaps. I had no doubt that there were in China and outside China many who privately equated the Communists with the alien Mongols and the Manchus. In the end China had reasserted its Chinaness over the outsiders. The Manchus and the Mongols became more Chinese than the Chinese whom they had conquered. Why should not the same thing happen again, and, with the passage of time, would not the Communists lose their rough edges, the hacking blade of raw national pride becoming smoothed and even burnished?

Time . . . China, I had always imagined, ran on a different kind of time than that recorded by Western clocks. Seventeen years had passed since Mao Tse-tung proclaimed the Communist regime in Peking. It seemed long to us. I wondered if it seemed more than a passing moment to the Chinese.

I had long been struck by the contrast between the Russian and the Chinese revolutions. In the first years after Lenin seized power Moscow became the mecca of Western intellectuals. H. G. Wells, Henri Barbusse, Emil Ludwig, all made the pilgrimage. The Bolsheviks thought of themselves not as Russians but as citizens of the world, and they believed it was only accidental that the revolution had been made in Russia—an accident of time, place and circumstance. It should have happened in Germany, and the Bolsheviks expected at any moment that it would happen in Germany. The Bolshevik languages were German and French and English. They had been educated in Geneva and Paris and Brussels. There were no barriers between them and the West. They *were* the West. Revolutionary Russia turned into a happy hunting ground for newspapermen and correspondents. Tourists and travelers wandered over the Russian land by the tens of thousands. Industrialists from New York and London and Berlin poured in on every train. Siemens built factories for Lenin. International Harvester put up tractor plants in Tsaritsyn—later to become Stalingrad. Thomas Campbell of Montana showed the Russians how to set up large-scale state wheat farms on irrigated acres. Colonel Hugh Cooper built the greatest dam in Russia at Dneprostroi. The Webbs wrote a two-volume work to prove that Russia under Stalin was becoming a socialist paradise.

But in China everything was different. Her borders, or so it seemed to me, had been sealed. Visitors, yes—but not any calculated to break down barriers between East and West—obscure men from Africa, an occasional writer from Chile, an eccentric or two from New Zealand. Trade? Until recently it had been almost all with Eastern Europe.

I saw that we were losing altitude now, and suddenly the plane dropped through the overcast, coming in low over tank farms, steel mills, the grease clouds of rubbish burning in the land fills—Tokyo; five Con Ed smokestacks belching pollution; neon signs gloaming in the haze—Jersey-in-Asia.

There was a brief pause and then the road again, this time down the China coast, but cautiously distant. I thought of Korea and how different that war had seemed to us and to the Chinese. To us China appeared aggressive, chauvinistic, dangerous. But to China the war had been a patriotic test of new nationhood and the results were a matter of national pride—a dramatic rebuff administered to the most powerful of the capitalist powers. I had no doubt that to the Chinese the attack on India's northern frontier seemed equally justified—evidence that China was now strong enough to right an ancient wrong, perpetrated by an historic enemy.

Did not this put the whole Chinese quarrel with Russia in an entirely different context? In Chinese eyes, who were the Russians? Just another white barbarian power which in the moment of China's great weakness in the nineteenth century assaulted her along with the other European powers—the English, the French, the Germans (and the Japanese). To the Chinese were not the Russians even worse than all the others since they hung grimly onto their acquisitions whereas the other powers long since had disgorged their conquests with the special exceptions of Hong Kong and Macao?

The world from Peking, it seemed to me, must assume a far different aspect than it did from Moscow or Washington.

I looked out the window. There was nothing to be seen but the rhythmically flashing red wing-tip lights, but somewhere beyond those lights lay the great mass of the China continent, dark, invisible, menacing. We flew on steadily. Then a quick swoop . . . a mountain of stars and a carpet of golden jewels in the velvet night—Hong Kong . . . China. . . .

I felt it was China the moment the car started to crawl through the narrow streets. It smelled like China. It sounded like China. Through each open, lighted shop front, beyond each curtained or uncurtained window, I saw China, bubbling, chattering, shouting, laughing, pushing. Chinese in the shops. Crowding the sidewalk. Jostling, peering, grinning. Chinese by the hundred, by the thousand, by the tens of thousands, by the million. Four million Chinese, living outside China. But not really outside. Their lives dependent on it. Their future bound to it. Their gods—Chinese. Their culture—Chinese. Their trade—Chinese. The biggest trading center on the Asian continent. Living, breathing, profiting, existing in union with China, tied as an unborn child to its mother, by the umbilical cord of mutual dependence. Four million Chinese. The entrepôt for 750 million more who lived just over the most distant hills.

And now the end of the Lo Wu Road was very close. A five-minute ferry ride across the harbor from Victoria to Kowloon; fishing junks, motorized with diesels from old London buses, endlessly churning the blue waters; American destroyers in gray battle dress; the Communist freighters, trailing red flags with five gold stars across the bulldog bows of the U.S. Navy; Star ferries hurrying on trips that never ended; the harbor ever in motion with the traffic of four million people and the hulking millions on the mainland behind them.

From Kowloon the road snakes past Nathan Road, jammed and turbulent. The khaki-shorted police saunter casually, with a quick eye for the street melees which flash up out of the turmoil of Hong Kong, the mysterious currents of Hong Kong politics, the cesspools of the Hong Kong underworld.

The road presses out into the New Territories (new areas on the mainland, leased at the turn of the century), the New Territories without which Hong Kong could not exist. Here is breathing space for the four million, but perilously little. And the calendar pitilessly signals the end of even this—and with it Hong Kong's end, perhaps. For the New Territories are held by lease, a ninety-nine-year lease which expires in 1997. With that date Hong Kong will also expire. Or will it? The four million seem indifferent. Thirty years to go. Enjoy it. Profit by it. Make it while you can. Anything can happen in thirty years. Look back ten years—the face of the city has been transformed. Hardly a remnant of the solid Victorian days except the square-block brownstone of the Hong Kong Club. (The signs— "Chinese and dogs not permitted"—long since vanished from the parks.) Now everything is glass and white façade and marble and cast-iron fretwork, a terraced Chinese San Francisco, the white towers of the offices and the twenty-story apartment buildings marching up the Peak and shadowing the elegance of the Repulse Bay Hotel. Building, building, building. More building than Los Angeles' Wilshire Boulevard—and looking very much like it.

Now the macadam highway leads through open country, beyond the golf courses and suburbia. There are farms here, rice paddies, vegetable patches, duck ponds. A sign beside the highway: "Lo Wu Road." It is a narrow gravel lane curving out and then against a hill. A yoke of oxen plods slowly ahead, and a half-mile down the road three Hong Kong policemen, neat in tan shorts and riding crops, halt the car and ask for passes. No one is allowed beyond this point without permission from the police commissioner. Two miles farther three more police officers check the passes. Now we have come to Lo Wu, 27 miles by road from Kowloon, 8,657 miles from New York, population 130, situated on the Shum Chum River. Across that river, no wider than Elm Creek, lies China.

Lo Wu . . . Gateway to China. The end of the road from the West. The beginning of the road to the East. By train it is 22 miles from Kowloon Central Station and 89 to Canton. Through this village flows China's intercourse with the world. In 1965 456,681 persons entered China from Lo Wu. Of these 11,400 were non-Chinese. The others were Chinese—mainland Chinese and overseas Chinese. Out of China emerged 475,192 persons via the Lo Wu Road. But not more than fifty a day were mainland Chinese seeking to enter Hong Kong as refugees. That is the number which is permitted entry. If more show up, the excess is turned back.

"Usually about fifty show up, sometimes a few less," says the very polite chief of the twelve-man police post. "Occasionally only four or five turn up. Then we know something has happened, but seldom what it is."

Lo Wu is a peaceful village. A British flag flies over the tan stucco station, a red Chinese flag over the train shed beyond the railroad bridge over the Shum Chum River. No trains cross the bridge. Four times a day the neat green-painted cars arrive from Kowloon. The passengers emerge and walk into the clean waiting room. They wait until the Canton train pulls in across the river at noon. Then the passengers for Hong Kong walk across to the Lo Wu side and the Canton passengers pick up their bags and walk down the tracks and across the bridge, where two Chinese Communist soldiers casually stand, Tommy guns strapped to their backs.

Above the Lo Wu waiting room the police have a small observation post. I stood on the tower and watched the Canton train come in. Twenty or thirty passengers, all Chinese except for half a dozen Europeans, walked across the bridge toward the Lo Wu station. I asked if I could take some pictures.

"Go ahead," the sergeant said. "But don't be surprised if they bring out a camera and start taking pictures of you."

"Why should they do that?" I asked.

"Who knows?" he said with a shrug of his shoulders. "But they do."

I took pictures of the Chinese watchtower, of the Chinese military barracks halfway up the hill on the other side of the river, of a dozen Chinese cultivating a collective farm just beyond the Shum Chum River, of the low train sheds and customs houses on either side, and of several humpy cows grazing on the China hillside.

Nothing happened. No Chinese rushed out with a camera. The soldiers with their Tommy guns glanced casually at the rooftop and then away.

A fortnight later a friend of mine crossed into China at Lo Wu. She asked the Chinese guard if it would be all right to take pictures of Lo Wu and the Hong Kong side.

"Sure," he said. "Go ahead. But don't be surprised if they come out and start taking pictures of you."

"Why would they do that?" she asked.

The Chinese shrugged his shoulders. "How do I know? All I know is that sometimes they do."

I stood on the clean concrete roof of the blockhouse and looked across to China. I might be looking anywhere. It didn't look sinister and it didn't look Chinese. I watched the farm people in the field. They were breaking up the earth with hoes, and down beside the Shum Chum River there was a youngster watching the humpbacked cows. The Hong Kong side looked just like the China side. Halfway up the hill back of Lo Wu station there was a cemetery, and sitting in the shade nearby was an old lady who had a dozen red ribbons spread in front of her—to be put on graves if anyone chanced to come that way. Just beyond her a dozen workers were shoveling gravel into a trench which had been dug as the foundation for a new freight shed. A Hakka woman with a hat that looked like a surrey with a fringe on top walked past. I asked the police captain whether it was always so peaceful.

"Not always," he said. Not a couple of years ago when the famine was on. Then the Chinese stormed across, broke down the barriers. That had been a very tense time. And, of course, there were peaks in travel. For instance, when the Peking Opera came to perform in Canton. Then, there might be ten or twenty or even thirty thousand people from Hong Kong who would go over for the performances. The Peking Opera was very popular with the Hong Kong Chinese.

But usually, he said, there wasn't much happening. A few Chinese were permitted to "commute" across daily. These were farmers who owned land in the New Territories. The Chinese Communists let them come over and work their farms. So did the Hong Kong authorities. At nightfall they went back to Communist China.

Here you are, I said to the officer, only a couple of hundred feet apart. Was there any kind of contact between the frontier guards on either side—did they sometimes sit down in the restaurant on the Chinese side or, perhaps, on the Hong Kong side and talk over a glass of beer?

The Hong Kong police captain smiled. No, there was never any conversation between the guards. That wasn't permitted. If any question arose, the procedure was for the captain to call his chief in Hong Kong. Hong Kong would pass the word to the commissioner, who in turn would inform the British chargé in Peking. The chargé would take the matter up with the Chinese Foreign Office. The Foreign Office would communicate with Canton, Canton would contact the Chinese guard post at Lo Wu, and the answer would come back through Peking and Hong Kong.

Supposing, I said, you had some urgent question. Is there any quicker way?

The captain shrugged his shoulders and patted his revolver in its shiny brown leather holster. Well, there was an alternate route and it was sometimes used. Sometimes they called the Hsinhua news agency in Hong Kong and told them the problem and Hsinhua informally passed the word to Peking.

But as for any contact across the barrier between the frontier police—no. That was not permitted.

I turned back to the landscape of China spread out before me. So that was it. The Lo Wu Road to China. It led to this tiny farm village, to the most peaceful, most pedestrian of landscapes. And this was the gateway, the entering point, the contact point for the largest nation in the world. It was, I thought, the very, very small end of a very large funnel. Was there any place around China's long frontier where there was more contact? I strongly doubted it.

To be sure, the traffic through Lo Wu was not small. It came close to half a million people annually. And yet this was a ridiculous number of people visiting a nation of 750 million. Some few more must come in by plane. There was a once-a-week Pakistan air service. But that would not bring in more than forty or fifty, I ventured to say. Did any come through Mongolia and Irkutsk? I doubted it. There might be a little traffic across the North Korean and the North Vietnamese frontiers. But this, too, must be a handful. What of the high Himalayas? Nepal had traffic with Tibet, but only freight went across that mountain road.

There was much nonhuman traffic across the Lo Wu barrier—34,577 freight cars of food passed from China into Hong Kong's New Territories last year. Very impressive. China, I knew, earned enough from the trade—about $500 million in hard currency—to finance most of her grain purchases. This, no doubt, was the key to the ambiguity of the Hong Kong–Chinese relationship. Hong Kong got its pork, its chicken, its eggs, its butter, its milk, its vegetables and much of its fruit from China. It was dependent on China for water. Cut the great main from China and Hong Kong would die almost overnight.

All along the eighteen miles of boundary that separated China from the New Territories there were strands of barbed wire and wooden towers from which the Communist Chinese and the Hong Kong Chinese watched each other. At any point along that frontier one side could shout and the other could answer. But from neither side was a voice raised. Each side mounted its guns, peered across the barbed wire and said nothing. And if there was a message to convey it went the long, long way around, via Hong Kong to Peking or via Canton to Peking and back.

In truth the Lo Wu Road was like a dead square on the parchisi board. You struggled to round the curve and when you finally succeeded you landed on a square which said: Go back three squares and wait an extra turn.

If even Chinese could not talk with Chinese at Lo Wu, how, I wondered, was it ever going to be possible to get a dialogue going between the West and Peking?

2
❋ A Chinese Dinner

I KNEW SOMETHING HAD GONE WRONG THE MOMENT OUR CHINESE friends appeared. He was a physician and she was a writer and while they lived in Hong Kong they were ardent supporters of the Peking regime.

"How would you like to meet some of our Chinese friends?" they had said when we spoke on the telephone that morning.

"Wonderful," I replied. I understood that the reference was to other sympathizers with Peking, possibly some Chinese who had just arrived from the mainland. Our friends said they would pick us up at the hotel, the big busy Hiltonish Mandarin which overlooks Hong Kong Harbor. Now, one glance at the faces of the couple as we met in the lacquered lobby told me that the evening somehow had gone awry. Badly. The enthusiasm of the morning had been replaced by something else. They were talking very rapidly and saying nothing. Nothing at all.

We walked down to the Star ferry, bought first-class tickets and rode over to Kowloon.

"We'll eat at our hotel," they said. "It's not far. We can walk."

The evening was breathless, the air quiet and the streets filled with people. The hotel was up toward Nathan Road. The crowds grew thicker. Shops were open. Cabarets and bars were going full blast.

Not until we sat down in a dining room that reminded me of the Chinese Republic Restaurant in Times Square did the subject of the "Chinese friends" come up.

"Our friends wouldn't come," the physician said. "They said they didn't want to meet any Americans right now."

It was the shooting down of the Chinese plane, they explained. That was the reason. The event was taken very seriously in Peking. I expressed my regret. The shooting had happened a couple of days earlier, and in spite of the headlines I really had not thought it more serious than some of the many other incidents. I went on to ask about a matter which troubled me far more—the crisis in Peking. What, I said, is behind the reports of purges, ideological disputes, attacks on "revisionists" and so on?

That, they said, is a serious matter, too. It shows that the enemies of the regime have not yet ceased to struggle, that there is still danger from within as well as from without. There had been attacks on diplomats, for instance. Two, in fact, and while it was said that the individuals who made the assault were deranged, could it not be possible that the attacks were part of a plot, possibly directed from inside China, and deliberately designed to stir up trouble against the regime?

I asked about Kuo Mo-Jo. How could this man, well into his seventies, a writer of great standing, the leading intellectual supporter of the regime, how could he revile everything he had written and say that all his works should be burned? What did it mean?

"You foreigners don't understand anything about China," the doctor's wife burst out. "Nothing bad will happen to Kuo. You Westerners are saying that he has been disgraced. It doesn't mean that at all. For instance, when I invite you to my house, I apologize for it, I say it is a poor mean house, that it really should be burned. I don't mean that literally. It is just our way of speaking."

She herself was a writer. She could well understand what Kuo Mo-jo meant. If she were in Peking she would say the same thing about her writings. Indeed, she had often made remarks like that.

Nothing she had written was of any value. It was trash. This had an entirely different meaning in Chinese.

"We aren't literal like you are," she said. "We make disparaging remarks as a way of showing modesty. Or perhaps of avoiding false pride."

There was undoubtedly much in what she said. But I doubted that this was all that was worrying her and her husband. Not by any means. The evening proceeded in disjointed fashion. The restaurant seemed to cater largely to tourists and non-Chinese. Violent discussions broke out between our hosts and the head waiter during the choice of the dishes. The manager was called for several times. As the dishes were brought, new arguments broke out. The courses were served in the wrong order. The soup came first instead of last, as is Chinese style. The serving plates were removed when they should have remained. They remained when they should have been taken away.

The doctor and his wife kept asking each other why they had come there. It was a question that puzzled me, too. Of all the excellent Chinese restaurants in Hong Kong why this miserable place? Had they chosen it because they were not likely to encounter friends there?

The couple occasionally visited in Peking. Outside of China they were known as warm supporters of the new regime. Inside China, I fancied, they might be regarded with mixed feelings. The China of today seemed to me to be more and more a black-and-white China. I wondered whether it still had room for people like these two, who so obviously had one foot in Hong Kong and the West, the other in Peking and the East.

The meal in the Chinese dining room with its nickel-plated fixtures, its bright neon lights, its swinging kitchen doors, its faint aura of Muzak and chow mein, seemed endless. Finally we got to the caramel apples. They were delicious—delicious enough so that the fact we had long since finished our soup did not seem to matter so much. The ordeal was over. We slipped out of the restaurant and sauntered slowly back to the Peninsular Hotel. In that relic of British colonialism we sat in a quiet corner on the balcony and had coffee and liqueurs.

Suddenly I found myself talking about the last days of Stalin —about the madness which came over the old dictator; about the plots which he invented as excuses for the purges; how he chose as his victims the men most closely associated with him; how the men in the Kremlin accommodated themselves to his insanity, played upon it, fed his sick, suspicious mind, trying to direct the paranoia in a manner to further their own desperate strivings for power.

"It grew worse as Stalin grew older." I said. "His vanity became overwhelming. He began to think of himself as immortal, and men who sought to curry his favor fed those vanities and conceits. It was an incredible time of terror, and the wonder is that Russia survived it."

This was a subject about which our friends could not hear enough. They wanted to know how Stalin's madness first manifested itself, what kind of persons were his victims. Hadn't the Party been able to stop him? I said that the first signs had been apparent many years earlier, certainly during the 1930's. But only after the war did the symptoms become so violent and bizarre. Generally, the victims were high members of the Party and intellectuals—writers and artists and, sometimes, scientists. Jews had been a favorite target. As for the Party—well, the Party was Stalin. No one could oppose him. His authority, prestige and power were too great.

As the talk went on I began to feel that their interest in Stalin's Russia was not vagrant curiosity—that my troubled Chinese friends were trying to fit against the background of what I was telling them about Stalin the events now transpiring in Peking. When we finally said good-bye and took the ferry to the Victoria side, the talk again was of regret over the savagery of American policy which was making it so difficult to maintain relations between Americans and Chinese. Not a word that possibly in Peking we might be witnessing some Chinese approximation of Stalin's fateful last days.

Charlotte and I went back to our hotel that night deeply troubled. We were fond of our Chinese friends. Very fond. They were warm, intelligent, sensitive, deeply concerned people, living in the most difficult of milieus, between the two polarly antagonistic worlds. Each tightening of the screw made life more difficult for them. Now, we felt, they were passing through a period of deep trauma, made deeper by the ritual frame of reference which seemed to make it impossible to discuss the real nature of events in Peking.

That a grave crisis now gripped Peking I had no doubt.

All Hong Kong was talking about it. Hong Kong is the center for China-watching. Here the diplomatic and intelligence services have concentrated their specialists. Here are scores of experts in every field of China affairs. They read the Chinese newspapers—including the provincial papers which are sometimes smuggled in by the Lo Wu Road, as packing material in crates of fruit. They tune in on Radio Peking (it blasts out so loud there is no avoiding it) and on dozens of provincial radio stations to see if the people in the capital and in the countryside are being told the same story. They talk to the Japanese businessmen who pass through Hong Kong at the rate of several thousand a year. They interview German technicians when they come back from three months' installing textile machinery in Lanchow or Changsha. They speak to the French-language teachers who leave Peking when their two-year contracts are up. They have private contacts among the thousands of Chinese who shuttle back and forth between Hong Kong and the mainland. They have access—or some do—to the espionage gathered by Chinese Nationalist agents who are set ashore by clandestine boats plying from Taiwan. And a few of the very top specialists receive the most revealing information of all: the technical and scientific data which are gathered every day, twenty-four hours a day, rain or shine, by the U.S. intelligence satellites whose courses crisscross China, seeing all, interpreting most and recording it on neat little photocards and

IBM tapes. If there is anything missing in this picture it can be filled in by the U-2 flights which the Chinese Nationalists obligingly conduct with only the occasional loss of one of our ingenious high-flying planes.

The life of a professional China watcher (like the life of a Kremlinologist or a forest ranger) is made up of days and weeks of tedious observation with little tangible result.

But now there was a full-blown crisis in Peking, so important, so all-embracing, so fundamental that the results would affect the whole balance of world relations.

Two things were happening. The *Liberation Daily*, the newspaper of the Chinese Communist Army, had suddenly sprung into prominence. Previously, it had been a mere echo of the Party paper, the Peking *People's Daily*. Now the *People's Daily* was taking its cue from the army paper, which was denouncing a series of cultural and political policies and figures, most of them centered around Peking. The whole Chinese press had launched a campaign to make what was called "the thought of Mao Tse-tung" the central motivation of every human endeavor.

For example, a vendor of vegetables in Peking had difficulty in selling his apples and onions. By applying the "thought of Mao Tse-tung" he found himself able not only to sell all his fruits and vegetables but had to order additional stocks. The "thought of Mao Tse-tung" enabled workers in a machine shop to solve a serious welding problem. It inspired border guards in Tibet to withstand 30-degree-below-zero cold and terrible blizzards.

The attacks upon Party and cultural leaders for harboring "bourgeois" tendencies and the embellishment of the achievements of simple people, accomplished by the study of the works of Mao, formed a common campaign.

It was in this campaign that Kuo Mo-jo had delivered his *mea culpa* and called on all writers to reinvigorate themselves by studying the thought of Mao and emulating the revolutionary deeds of the people.

What did this mean and who was behind it? If I could learn

this it would cast great light on the question that had propelled me across the Pacific: What is motivating China, what does she want in the world, what is the meaning of the strange and menacing statements from Peking? Among the China watchers there was no clear consensus. Most of them started from the point that there must be a struggle for power in Peking. But they did not agree on who was involved and the role of the leading Chinese Party members.

"We all start out with Mao," one American said. "Is he ill? Dead? Has he had a stroke which has left him incapacitated? We don't know. We can only guess. And this tells you a good deal about the uncertainty of China-watching. When you realize that on this single, central point, this vital element in any assessment, we have no real information and can only guess, you can see what we are up against."

For example, he said, a diplomat had come through Hong Kong only the week before with "positive information" that Mao had suffered a stroke in December and now five months later was still unconscious.

"But when you pinned him down," the American said, "it was just a rumor."

Lack of real knowledge had not prevented many China watchers from concluding that Mao no longer was playing an active role in China's affairs and that among his close associates a fierce struggle had broken out for the power slipping from his feeble hands.

To back this hypothesis, the China watchers pointed out that Mao had appeared in public with increasing infrequency. During all of 1965 he had not been seen more than three or four times. Diplomats and newsmen from Peking thought he seemed increasingly feeble. He had not been present on the great October 1, 1965, holiday in Tien An Men (Heavenly Peace) Square. This is the anniversary of the proclaiming of power of the Chinese Revolution. He had appeared on the podium on May 1. True, there had been past occasions when he was not present on October 1. True, he had made a practice in recent years of going to the south in order to escape Peking's fierce autumn winds. Nonetheless, his only appearance in the last six months which could be pointed to with some assurance was his attendance at a birthday reception for Anna Louise Strong, the elderly American supporter of the China regime. On her eightieth birthday, November 24, he arranged for Miss Strong and a group of her friends to be flown to a point (unspecified in the accounts but probably Wuhan). There he attended the birthday reception and Miss Strong duly recorded the event in her monthly "Letter from China."

Since that time no one had seen Chairman Mao.

Among the many rumors a favorite was that Mao was in a sanatorium or rest home somewhere outside of Shanghai.

This report usually was coupled with another. Lin Piao, one of the most evangelical of Mao's associates, was said to be staying in the same rest house near Shanghai. Lin Piao had been seen in public even less frequently than Mao. His health had been delicate since the late 1930's, when he was severely wounded in fighting against the Japanese, and he was said to suffer from a mild tuberculosis. But this was merely incidental to the theory that Lin Piao was Mao's chosen successor and was, in fact, presiding over the decline of the Chinese Chairman.

Interest in Lin Piao had been growing since September, 1965, when he published a remarkable paper to mark the twentieth anniversary of the defeat of Japan in World War II.

This article was entitled "Long Live the Victory of the People's War."

What Lin presented here was a prescription for achieving world revolution by applying the tactics of Mao Tse-tung's Long March. When the Communists were defeated in the Chinese cities in 1925 by Chiang Kai-shek, who seized power and turned on his erstwhile Communist associates, Mao (in violation of every teaching of Marx) retreated to the villages and the vast Chinese countryside. There, fighting occasional guerrilla actions, he built up his strength very slowly and when severely harassed retreated even deeper into the countryside—during the famous Long March of the 8th Route Army to Yenan. His tactic was never to accept battle with a superior force but constantly to harass and nibble away.

Mao's tactics worked. It took twenty-five years, but by 1949 the Communists had become supreme in China.

Lin applied this lesson to the world scene. He compared the revolutionary movements in Vietnam to Mao's forces in 1925. Gradually, he said, they would gain the upper hand. And not only in Vietnam. The same guerrilla revolutionaries, the same tactics of the "People's War," would be victorious throughout the world. The native revolutionaries of Asia, Africa and Latin America would slowly gain ascendency and in the end "surround" the citadel of advanced capitalism in North America and Europe.

"Everything is divisible," said Lin. "And so is this colossus of U.S. imperialism. It can be split up and defeated. The peoples of Asia, Africa, Latin America and other regions can destroy it piece by piece, some striking at its head and others at its feet."

There were some China watchers who thought Lin Piao's article might be the most important revolutionary document of the second half of the twentieth century. With this I agreed.

To me there seemed to be a Thermidorian character to the polemical literature which was coming out of Peking. It had a shrillness, an almost maniacal tone, as though its authors were in a frenzy to save the Revolution from imminent danger of bourgeois pollution.

It might be true that Mao was in dubious health and was fading from the scene as his would-be heirs quarreled over the succession. It might be that Lin Piao was staking out his claim against the challenge of Teng Hsiao-ping, Party Secretary General, and Peng Chen, the dynamic Mayor of Peking.

But I could not help remembering the last months of Stalin's regime. There was much we did not yet know about that fateful period. But enough of the curtain had been lifted to show that the man who was manipulating the stage, selecting the victims for the new plot, inspiring the polemics and winding the machinery of the clockwork characters was not someone acting for Stalin or behind Stalin's back. It was Stalin himself.

Might this not be true of China? Was it not very much in the character of aging dictators to clutch at any mechanism to hold back the passage of time? Did they not feel more strongly than anyone else the break between generations, the changing of the guard, the inevitable betrayal by men younger than they, men who did not share their sense of and passion for the purity of the revolutionary ideal?

I thought of a conversation I had had several months before with a Westerner who had spent a short time in Peking. He told me of a meeting which he had there with a cultured Chinese who held a minor post in the regime. The Chinese was explaining the Party's attitude toward the Vietnam war.

"Perhaps," he said, "we may be drawn into it. And perhaps it would not be altogether a bad thing."

He explained that China had a new generation of young people, grown up in a world transformed from that of the Long March, unaware of the meaning of hunger, exhaustion, danger, sweat, toil and sacrifice.

"Every revolution," he said, "sooner or later comes to a crossroads. It must make a choice. One road leads back to capitalism, to other goes forward to Communism."

No longer, he said, could the younger generation in China be trusted to make the right decision.

"If war comes to us over Vietnam," he said, "it will be hard. Very hard. People will suffer. People will die. But our young people will be saved. They will learn what it means to make a revolution, to be a Communist."

Not all Communists make the right decision, he said sadly. For instance, Yugoslavia and the Soviet Union. They had taken the wrong turn—the one that led back to capitalism.

There might, indeed, I thought, be a struggle for power under way in Peking. But was it not a struggle led by Mao? Was it not possible that the aging dictator was fighting his last battle? A struggle not to gain power but to hold it; not for temporal but for spiritual control; not for here and now but to fasten upon future generations the doctrine of Yenan, the pure revolutionary spirit crystallized in those distant difficult days. Was it not possible that Mao was thinking not of the present but of the long centuries of China's future? Could he not be trying to establish himself as the new Confucius? Was he, in a sense, acting as his own Paul of Tarsus? Or was that the role in which Lin Piao was cast?

It was not yet possible to be certain of all this, but before my orbit of China was completed the evidence had begun to pile up. By the day in late July when Mao "once again had a good swim in the Yangtze" the verdict was clear for all to read.

Just as Mao had, in the eyes of his dedicated colleagues, bravely breasted the waves and storms of the great river, just as he had correctly estimated his own force relative to that of the Yangtze, so had he spelled out the lesson to China. It was: Strengthen yourself, be ready to bear any hardship, remember that a brave man can stand up against any odds.

And if there were any doubt that Mao's struggle was for the heart and soul of the younger generation of Chinese, this too was made plain when the teen-age "Red Guards" were set loose in the streets of Peking to demand that the traffic lights be changed so that red signaled "Go" and green "Stop"; to rename the great Peking Square from "Heavenly Peace" to "East Is Red"; to smash stamp collectors' shops as "bourgeois"; to break into people's homes and toss out nonrevolutionary pointed shoes and sports shirts; to blackguard the police themselves into changing their names to "Red Guards"—as raging, as untrammeled, as naïve an example of revolutionary energetics as could be conceived.

Its purpose? A foreign Communist, a Peking supporter, watching the violent action approved it all for it would, he said, "give the youth a revolutionary experience which they will treasure all their lives."

One day the Red Guards broke into Peking's Roman Catholic church, tore the crucifix from the altar and set up a plaster bust of Mao. The meaning could not be made more plain. Before the eyes of the world a new God of China was in the process of creation.

3

Plowing the Sacred Furrow

THE SUN BEAT DOWN ON THE FIELD WHERE THE CROWDS HAD GATHERED
to watch the gray bullocks pull the plow through the heavy red
soil. Solemnly and quietly the peasants stood while the great beasts
strained and tugged at the command of a chubby man who followed
behind. Slowly the oxen dragged the heavy plow across the paddy
field of Svay Rieng until they reached the far side, where the
wooden yokes were lifted from their necks and before them were
set bowls of maize, of rice, of soya, of water and of wine.

The beasts plunged their muzzles into the corn, then turned to
the rice and the soya. They drank some water and lifted up their
heads, leaving the wine untouched.

A grin spread over the round face of Prince Sihanouk and a cheer
rose from the crowd. Once again as for a thousand years past the
ancient rite of the sacred plowing of the earth had been accomplished and the omens were good.

Prince Sihanouk mopped a trace of sweat from his brow and
turned to his people. He began to talk easily and earnestly and
lengthily.

Not a dozen miles from the plowed field the Vietnam war blazed
on. Cambodia's relations with the United States teetered perilously
on the edge of crisis. The danger of invasion—or so Prince Sihanouk
was convinced—by South Vietnam and Thailand grew each day.

He had broken relations with the United States, embraced a policy of positive neutrality and announced Cambodia's reliance on her "No. 1 friend," China. But despite all this the threat of Cambodian involvement seemed more and more grave. But first things first. For uncounted centuries the spring fertility rite had symbolized the social unity of the people, their land, their beasts and their monarch. Once again it had been performed and the signs were very good indeed. Perils might rage beyond the frontier and trouble might beset the land. But the beasts had signed that there would be a fine crop of maize, plenty of rice, a sufficiency of soya and enough water to keep Cambodia's lands tenderly green. What more could one ask?

It was not like the terrible spring of 1959—the year the beasts drank wine! The worst of all omens! Portent of drought, of catastrophe, of tragedy. So it had proved in 1959. That year three plots to overthrow Prince Sihanouk had been uncovered, including one which came perilously close to succeeding and another in which the court chamberlain and one of the Prince's sons were killed by a bomb wrapped up as a birthday gift to the Queen.

The memory of the year the beasts drank wine burned in the consciousness of the Prince and his people. They were one in their belief that the CIA had been behind the three plots, and they were ever on guard against a repetition.

A month after the festival of the sacred furrow Charlotte and I drove through the lovely fields of Svay Rieng. The rice was being set out from the nursery beds, the corn was rising nicely, water filled the irrigation ditches and the paddies looked rich and prosperous.

But it was not to admire agricultural abundance that we had come to Svay Rieng. We came to inspect some of the wounds and scars which the Vietnam war had graven on the graceful Cambodian people; to get some measure of the damage the conflict has inflicted upon countries which the ill luck of geography had placed in its neighborhood.

Just after the plowing of the sacred furrow another event occurred in Svay Rieng. A battalion of American troops, part of Big Red One, the 1st Infantry Division, had been making a sweep along the Vietnam side of the Cambodian border, methodically mopping up War Zone C, one of the strongholds of the Vietcong.

The drive, called Operation Birmingham, was progressing well. Considerable stocks of materials had been found cached near the frontier and a fair number of Vietcong were being flushed out.

On April 29 an American battalion was moving north on a jungle road, a quarter to a half mile east of the Caibac River, which forms the Viet-Cambodian frontier at that point. The American unit worked its way roughly opposite the Cambodian village of Tros, when it was fired on apparently from both the Viet and the Cambodian sides of the river.

The Americans made camp on the night of the twenty-ninth a mile and a half north of Tros. The next morning they went upriver toward an abandoned Vietnam village named Lo Go.

Almost immediately they drew very heavy fire, which the American commander felt certain came from the Cambodian side of the Caibac River. Believing he had encountered a typical Vietcong L-shaped ambush with the long side on the Cambodian frontier and the short side in Lo Go, he ordered his artillery to shell the Cambodian shore. He then observed, or so he later reported, Vietcong crossing the Caibac River and taking refuge on the Cambodian side. He promptly laid three hundred more shells onto Cambodian soil.

This deliberate reprisal on Cambodia by the Americans—the first such of the war—sharpened the crisis in Cambodian-U.S. relations. There was talk of all-out American action to wipe out the "privileged sanctuary" of the Vietcong in Cambodia. It was to investigate this affair that Charlotte and I arrived in Svay Rieng on a hot morning in early June. It was typical of the confusion of the place and time that six weeks had gone by without anyone either from the outside or from the central Cambodian Government going to the scene to find out what lay behind the occurrence at Lo Go. At Svay

Rieng we got into jeeps and, escorted by provincial military officials, set out along the cattle tracks and jungle trails toward the frontier.

We quickly found that we had not one incident to investigate but half a dozen. In each little village there was a story of strafing by planes—often repeated strafing. The big American operation—the villagers called it *"une grande manoeuvre américaine"*—had begun about April 21. The Cambodians knew it had started because they heard heavy firing on the frontier and saw flight after flight of American jets and helicopters.

Soon they not only saw the American planes; they felt the weight of American fire. At Kompong Batras three jets and one observation plane appeared on April 24, dropped a bomb and hastened on.

At the nearby Kompong Trach frontier command post, five miles west of Kompong Batras, five helicopters appeared at 11 P.M., April 25. They hovered over the post for some minutes, dropping magnesium flares and firing random machine-gun and rocket bursts. Each night for four nights the copters reappeared and dropped flares. The Cambodian commander concluded that the Americans must have suspected that his barracks was a Vietcong staging area. He showed us where an American shell had plowed into the barracks kitchen. In a nearby field a burst of rocket fire had killed two cows. Fearing the air activity might be preliminary to an attack across the frontier, the commander put his forces and the militia on the alert. Among the alerted posts was Peam Metrey on the Caibac River bank, seven miles south of Tros. The Peam Metrey commander showed us how he had spelled out the name of his post in wooden blocks along the river bank just at the junction of the Caibac and Cai Cai rivers. Then he led us to a barracks and pointed out where American rocket bursts had plowed through the roof. Fortunately no one had been hit. He also showed us an unexploded bomb which had been recovered from a nearby field.

We then drove north on a narrow road that roughly paralleled the Caibac River. It led through open irrigated rice fields. Here and there the savanna opened to the river, giving a clear view of

Vietnam on the other side. The country was well settled. Seldom were we out of sight of farms. Tracks led through the forest patches to the river banks, and villagers, often on bicycles, moved along the river road or in and out of the forest tracks. It was obvious that neither Vietcong guerrillas nor organized units could maneuver in this countryside without instant detection by the Cambodians.

Seven miles north of Peam Metrey the road entered a clearing surrounded by pastures and a succession of rice fields leading eastward toward the river. A bit to the west we could see thatched houses, sheltered under groves of palm and banana trees. In the foreground gray cattle were grazing. This was Tros, scene of the incident involving the Americans.

Chief Sergeant Neany Im of the local frontier guard, a brisk, soldierly young man with a neat notebook, led us over the ground. He showed us the jungle patch alongside an open pasture where most of the American shells fell. I picked up a jagged shard of shrapnel and took pictures of the splintered trees which bore the brunt of the bombardment.

Then we picked our way through rice fields to the banks of the Caibac. Here Neany Im showed us well-dug foxholes concealed behind trees along the river bank. Here he and his militia contingent of half a dozen men had been on guard on the morning of April 30. They had been at their posts for several days because of the noisy activity on the Vietnam side of the Caibac—not more than twenty yards wide at this point.

They heard firing the afternoon before, and there had probably been firing onto the Cambodian side and possibly return fire (although no one was very clear about that) on the afternoon of the twenty-ninth. No troops, the villagers insisted, had been seen on the Vietnam shore. The river edge was heavily forested, but just opposite Tros there was a cleared patch which looked like a landing stage. It was obviously the sort of thing which a search-and-destroy party of American troops would investigate.

"Didn't any troops come down there?" I asked.

They insisted they had seen none.

The next morning at about 8 A.M. all hell burst loose. Shells came whamming overhead from the Vietnam side. The villagers jumped into their foxholes. Cheay Peao, an excitable young villager who manned the only machine gun, opened fire at the opposite bank. Others joined in with their rifles.

Why had they opened up? They thought they were being attacked. They did not aim at anything. Nothing was to be seen. They just fired into the jungle.

The exchange went on for twenty minutes. There was another outburst about noon. At no time, the villagers insisted, did they see anyone—neither Americans nor Vietcong. No one crossed the river. If anyone had, they would have fired at him.

There wasn't much more to the story. Not all the villagers agreed on details. Several insisted the river was filled with alligators and too swift for a man to swim. This seemed doubtful. I thought it would provide no obstacle to a desperate Vietcong hard pressed by American pursuers. I could not help wondering why no one had been seen at the landing stage.

The villagers said the second burst of American shelling was directed at another dense jungle patch north of the village. No one was hurt, no one was wounded, no huts were damaged, no cattle were hit. Could the Vietcong have taken refuge in the jungle north of the village? Absolutely not, the villagers said. I did not feel 100 percent certain of that myself. But I did not see how any Viet units could long remain on the Cambodian side without being detected. The idea I had brought from America of an "impenetrable jungle" did not match this easily penetrable tangle of wood and undergrowth.

The American commander reported two of his men were killed by fire from the Cambodian side. He gave the locale as somewhat north of Tros. But, I wondered, could not this have been the result of random firing by the Tros militia? There was no way for the Americans to know who was firing on them from the Cambodian side. The foxholes were invisible under cover of the riverside vegetation.

We went back to the village of Tros. A rather dreary village it was. Some eight hundred inhabitants. A run-down temple. Nothing but huts and small enclosures for cattle. Thunderclouds came up in the sky. It was late afternoon and sweltering hot. We paused a moment to say good-bye to the villagers. Suddenly, I saw them freeze. For a moment I did not understand. Then I heard it, too— the distant drone of a plane high in the cloud cover. We stood, all listening. The villagers were poised for flight. Then the engine's sound grew fainter and fainter. The villagers relaxed, went on about their business. We got into the jeep and began the long, rugged journey back over the border tracks to Svay Rieng. It was mid-evening before we drew up at the Governor's Palace, a fairyland with lights of red and blue and green and amber, sparkling in the mango trees. Inside we relaxed under the lazy ceiling fans and drank from ice-chilled glasses. Presently, refreshed, we sat down to dinner at a long mahogany table, strewn with camellias and set with sparkling silver.

In the distance there was an intermittent rumble and the crystal gently tinkled against the silver. For a moment I thought it was summer thunder.

"It's the bombing," Governor Ou Tong Hao said quietly. "It's been going on now for more than a year. Almost every night. Do you wonder that we sometimes fear the bombs will fall on us?"

"Will the bombs fall on us?" This was the question, I quickly found, which so deeply concerned Cambodians. It was put in many forms.

"What can we do?" the Premier, Prince Norodom Kantol, asked me. "We have tried again and again to demonstrate the falsity of the propaganda against us. We invite everyone to inspect our frontiers. We beg them to assure themselves of our neutrality."

The Prince, a gentle man, took a cambric handkerchief from his breast pocket and dabbed at the corners of his eyes.

"Excuse me," he said. "I know I should not feel this so strongly. But it is so discouraging. It seems that no matter what we do no one believes us. How can we keep war away from our country? That is all we want."

I pointed out that it was difficult for Americans to consider that Cambodia was neutral when she broke diplomatic relations with the United States, expelled all Americans from the country and proclaimed China as her "No. 1 friend."

But, insisted Prince Kantol, people do not seem to understand. Cambodia had not wanted to break relations with the United States. Quite to the contrary. But again and again the Vietnamese, the South Vietnamese, violated Cambodia's frontiers. Cambodia complained. Nothing happened. The United States refused to intervene, yet South Vietnam was under U.S. domination.

No one, the Prince said, seemed to realize that Vietnam was Cambodia's traditional enemy. They had fought war after war, the Cambodians and the Annamites. So had the Thais and the Cambodians. Even today the Vietnamese and the Thais were deep in a plot to obliterate Cambodia from the map, to assault her from east and west, and divide her sacred soil along the line of the Mekong River. Perhaps the Americans did not understand this. Perhaps the Americans were merely being used. But it was this deep, undying hostility of the Vietnamese and the Thais which lay behind the friction, the border incidents, the charges and countercharges, the propaganda which associated Cambodia with the Vietcong. The fact was, the Prince said, that Cambodia had no more love for the Vietnamese who lived in the North than those in the South. For the moment relations with North Vietnam were friendly. This was because North Vietnam respected Cambodia's frontiers. But if at the end of the war there emerged but one Vietnam, Cambodia would have to be on guard, regardless of whether Vietnam's capital was Hanoi or Saigon.

Cambodia's friendship with China, the Prince said, was "sentimental," not strategic. Cambodia was not taking sides between East and West. China had done nothing bad to Cambodia. Cambodia needed a friend and she had China. That was all there was to it.

Son Sann, the aristocratic Privy Counselor of Prince Sihanouk, chief of the Central Bank, a conservative man to whom Paris is a second home (and Peking never could be), pointed out that the Cambodian fears of attack by their traditional enemies had a foundation in reality. Under the sponsorship of the South Vietnamese a "Khmer Serai" or Cambodian Freedom movement had been launched utilizing Cambodian nationals resident in South Vietnam. About six hundred men had been armed and trained with the help of the U.S. Special Forces, a branch of the CIA. The Khmer Serai first had been used in forays along the Cambodian-Vietnamese frontier. More lately units had been flown in U.S. planes to Thailand and put into action on the Thai-Cambodian frontier. Possibly the top-echelon American command and diplomats were not aware of what was going on at lower levels. But the evidence was indisputable. Many Khmer Serai had been captured by the Cambodians and readily told how they were recruited, where they were trained and how the Americans had participated.

I found, on investigation, that Son Sann's allegations were true. I talked with some of the captured Khmer Serai and with informed American diplomats who showed no inclination to deny the charges, although they did minimize them, contending that American influence was being used to calm the adventurous Thais and Vietnamese.

It was this kind of buccaneering by the United States and particularly its intelligence agencies, it was clear, which had driven Prince Sihanouk to attempt to utilize China as a protecting power.

So far as men like Son Sann and Prince Kantol were concerned, I was convinced this was simply a matter of attempting to give Cambodia some balance in a dangerous world. But there were others in the Prince's entourage who viewed the matter in different terms. Cambodia is, in Prince Sihanouk's own words, a country of "socialisme buddhistique," or Sangkum. Among his advisers are men who see this as only a transitional stage en route to "socialisme communistique," à la Peking. To these men the "friendship" with

China has meant something quite different than to Son Sann, Prince Kantol and to Prince Sihanouk himself.

These are the men who have publicly said: "If Cambodia calls, China will come." They mean by this the Chinese Liberation Army. It will come, they insist, whatever the reason for the call—aggression by Thailand, South Vietnam or the United States itself. If this plunges Asia into nuclear war—well, let it.

It is not only in the United States that the Prince's quixotic actions have stirred a measure of distrust. In the autumn of 1965 in the full bloom of his friendship with China the Prince embarked on a grand tour of the Communist world. First, he went to Peking. His second stop was Pyongyang in North Korea. From there his itinerary included Moscow, Warsaw and the other capitals of Eastern Europe.

The first stop was Peking. There he threw himself into the arms of Mao Tse-tung and, as only he can, delivered a flamboyant speech emphasizing Cambodia's eternal friendship for China. He even wrote a special song for his visit, called "Nostalgia for China." Then he went on to Pyongyang. It is possible that Sihanouk had some intimation that his Peking remarks might not have made the most pleasant impression in Moscow, where the very name of Mao was anathema. His first act on reaching the Korean capital was to hand over to the Soviet Ambassador the text of the speech he proposed to deliver at Moscow airport, ostensibly so that it could be translated into Russian (the Prince proposed to deliver his remarks in Russian) but actually, no doubt, to show the Soviet that in his big heart there was room for friendship for both Russia and China.

An evening or two before he was due to depart for Moscow the Soviet Ambassador demanded an immediate audience. Sihanouk's aides tried to put him off. He insisted that he must see the Prince immediately. A few minutes later he strode into the Prince's suite, smoking a big cigar. He flung himself down in an armchair, reached into his pocket, extracted what the Prince later described as a "dirty piece of paper" and tossed it on the table with the gruff remark: "I'm instructed to give you this."

The "dirty piece of paper" turned out to be a dis-invitation.

Moscow advised Sihanouk that the moment was not appropriate to receive him.

The Prince seems to have been stunned by the Soviet action. He called off his tour of the Communist world. Instead, he went back to Peking, spent a few more days with his Chinese friends and then returned to Phnompenh, where he called a great public meeting at which he described in vivid detail what had happened.

Having treated Sihanouk to a thorough drenching with cold water, the Russians sedulously set about re-establishing good relations, a task which took many months. But by the time of our arrival good terms had been restored and there were signs that the Prince was shifting Cambodia's course back toward more of a middle of the road position.

There were sound reasons for such a change. By her neutrality policy Cambodia had renounced all foreign aid except small Soviet and Chinese projects. These came nowhere near the level of the huge American commitments before the 1963 break. No longer did Cambodia's army receive U.S. equipment (and training). Phnompenh itself suffered a grievous blow when at one fell swoop eighteen hundred Americans quit the country, leaving behind them such a plunge in the real estate market and retail trade that the city had not yet recovered. Cambodia's upper classes lived well on the prosperity of American aid. Like so many of their peers in Southeast Asia, they had become accustomed to the Mercedes, the frequent trips to Paris, the *couturière* clothes, the luxury villas. There was no hope for that kind of "skim" from the spartan Chinese and Russian aid projects. The generals were restive, too. The American equipment was fine, but there wasn't enough. It was growing obsolete and what about spare parts? No hope that Russia or China could fill the gap. French officers still conducted training missions, but they were not forthcoming with materiel.

For a time Sihanouk turned his back on his No. 1 friend and his worrisome enemies alike. He flung his energies into something entirely different—a movie! Nothing over the years had bothered

Sihanouk more than what he considered the false image of Cambodia held in foreign countries. He decided to make a film to show Cambodia as it really was. And, to be certain that it met his intentions, he decided to write the script, direct the picture, edit it and produce it himself.

As the star of the picture he picked Princess Bopha Devi, one of the most beautiful of his daughters, the premiere ballerina of the Royal Ballet Cambodge. He titled his picture *Apsara*, for Cambodia's traditional "heavenly dancers." The plot revolved around a young girl forced by her family to marry an older man. Eventually all turns out well and she is united with her young lover. For actors the Prince drew on his court and cabinet. Most of his ministers played roles. So did the generals and air force. Cambodia's jet striking force—all eight planes—was committed to the picture. So was most of the army, despite the threatening situations on the eastern frontiers.

Finally, all was ready. The Prince invited the diplomatic corps to a premiere. Some diplomats said later it was the longest picture they had ever seen. The Prince took note of the length. In its full version, he said, it would be entered in the film festivals of the Eastern world—Moscow and Karlovarie. But for Cannes it would be cut. For instance, a half-hour belligerent speech by his Defense Minister berating the "Western imperialists" would be deleted. He was so enchanted with his handiwork that he could hardly wait to embark upon another picture—also to be written, produced, directed and edited by himself. There would be one difference in the new picture. The Prince would also play the title role.

Some diplomats felt the Prince was retreating from reality, taking refuge in a dream world and letting the urgent problems of his kingdom drift. But this did not really seem to be the case. Prince Sihanouk is a compulsive man, a compulsive eater (he goes into a hospital each year for three weeks to reduce and get back into physical shape), a compulsive drinker, a compulsive talker. His whims are monumental and his interest in himself and his own activities infinite. His life is lived like a constant newsreel before the eyes of his delighted subjects, who fondly call him "The Prince who once was King." He publishes a monthly magazine called *Cambodge.* On its cover he proudly imprints the words "Manager: Norodom Sihanouk." In it he publishes almost every letter he receives and writes. He also publishes clippings from foreign newspapers about himself and his kingdom (together with refutations of what he considers to be misstatements and libels). In Phnompenh he has created a Prince Sihanouk Museum which is filled with artifacts concerning himself: two Tommy guns he got as a present from the Soviet Union, the revolver the Vietcong gave him, the letter from Mrs. Eisenhower thanking him for his inaugural gift, a letter from President Johnson enclosing the first satellite pictures of the moon, his school report card (the grades: all A's), the furniture from his father's bedroom in the palace (very splendid), the furniture from his mother's bedroom (very simple), a letter of appreciation from the movie starlet whom he crowned Beauty Queen of Asia at a Singapore contest (she was so thrilled to meet a "real prince"), keys to the cities of San Francisco, Detroit and Calcutta, and two accordions, one the present of a man named Buddy in the United States.

"It is easy to make fun of Sihanouk," the foreign minister of a neighboring state told me later. "He is eccentric. And, frankly, he fills me with antagonism. But I cannot help but admire him. For ten years he has held the center of the stage with nothing but a tiny nation behind him—and his brains. I never underestimate him. Particularly when he is doing something which seems to make no sense at all."

The Prince heads a country of a little more than six million population. Almost half of these are non-Cambodians—Chinese or Vietnamese—and a few—very few—Thais. This is not much matched against Vietnam's 30 million and Thailand's 26 million. But—and this is an eternal debt which Cambodia owes to France—by the mid-nineteenth century when France appeared in Indochina Cambodia was down to less than 500,000 and she was on the verge of extinction as a nation.

But the odds are still enormous. Sihanouk has an army of 30,000 men. Vietnam has a million men under arms, roughly divided half and half between North and South—not to mention 350,000 or more Americans. And to the west Thailand disposes another 500,000 fighting men.

To keep a small state alive against these odds is no mean trick. Possibly only the eccentricities of Sihanouk would succeed. Possibly even the eccentricities will not.

In the face of such odds did it make sense to suppose Sihanouk was playing fast and loose with the Vietcong and the North Vietnamese? I did not think so in spite of the earnest assurances which I later was to hear in Vientiane about the "Sihanouk trail" and the deal under which Sihanouk was supposed to have agreed to provide thirty thousand tons of rice to the Vietcong. It made no sense in view of Cambodia's short rice crop and the urgent need which she had for foreign exchange to tide her over the hard times imposed by the loss of U.S. aid.

The talk of the Sihanouk trail made even less sense when matched against the reality of trade between Cambodia and Vietnam. One did not have to leave Phnompenh to learn that smuggling, as might be expected, had been vastly stimulated by the war. But it was following no mysterious Sihanouk trails through the jungles and mountains of northern Cambodia. It was following the traditional routes of the Mekong. The goods were pouring down Route Nationale No. 1, the main French-built highway between Phnompenh and Saigon. There was an open uninhibited flow across the frontier, handled for the most part by the smuggling merchants, mostly Chinese and Vietnamese, through their long-established connections in Saigon and Phnompenh. Thousands of Phnompenh residents drove down to the Svay Rieng frontier every weekend to buy cheap American goods, whiskey, cigarettes, nylons, soap, cosmetics, the usual run of PX goods. Trade going the other way was mostly foodstuffs, including much rice. Was it going to the Vietcong? Certainly—so long as they were willing to pay the price. The smuggling fraternity in Saigon didn't care who bought so long as they had hard cash. Lately the Cambodian currency had been growing firmer, an unlikely development in view of Cambodia's economic difficulties. But the explanation was simple. Cambodian dealers were getting paid for their smuggled rice with direct deposits of dollars in Hong Kong. Pressure on the riel was automatically reduced.

"Of course there is smuggling on the border," the Cambodians said. "There always has been. We try to stop it. But really the Vietnamese are far better able to stop it than we are. They have 500,000 men in their army. We have 30,000. And what about those merchants in Saigon who are growing rich on the trade? Is that our fault?"

They had a point, I thought. But I wondered whether reason and logic made much difference in this situation. As the atmosphere heated up, it was not reality that mattered so much as the growing distortions from reality which were accepted by people as being true.

Alone among the leaders of Southeast Asia Sihanouk had sought to steer his country through troubled waters, guided by the beacon of neutrality and fixing his hopes on what he saw as the protective power of distant China. Would it be enough? The further I got from Phnompenh, the more I wondered. Cambodia was a land so beautiful, a land in which the people, the animals and their life seemed to possess such unity, that I could not bear to think of it being smashed to bits, turned into a bloody junk heap by American bombs, dropped by our own pilots or those of the nations with whom we had cast our lot.

Cambodia, certainly, wanted little enough. She wanted to live in peace. She wanted no part in our war. Nor that of anyone else. Was this too much to ask? So it might well be in the Southeast Asia of the middle 1960's.

I could not erase from my mind the image of an evening at

Angkor Wat and the Cambodian dancers gently swaying on the ancient stone terrace under an Asian moon. Slender and delicate (all the dancers are young women) Prince Rama drew his wooden sword and vanquished his sorcerer adversary. Then he offered his arm to his fairy bride, took her by her flower-wreathed arm and led her to his palace.

So the dance was performed at the court of King Suryavarman more than eight hundred years ago; so it is done today by the Royal Ballet of Cambodia at the court of Prince Sihanouk.

Nothing—nothing—could be more gentle, more eternal, more redolent of tranquillity and bounty; nothing so remote from war than this island of peace, island of neutrality, island of nonalignment, island of *socialisme buddhistique* where the warring princes are really charming girls and the most dangerous weapon is a wooden wand. How long, I wondered, could it thus endure? And if it fell, on whom would the blame descend—Prince Sihanouk with all his eccentricities, the Chinese with their nascent, almost adolescent, ambitions or ourselves, powerful, hopeful but goliath-like in the application of our incredible power?

4
The Chinese Tails

WE WERE SITTING ON THE TERRACE OF THE ORIENTAL HOTEL IN Bangkok, watching a woman maneuver her water taxi across the fast-moving Chao Phraya River. She took two steps forward, then a step back, two forward, one back. It was like the opening movements in a ballet. Somehow, she held the sweeping oar so that the current caught it and the small boat bounced across the stream almost in a straight line.

My Chinese friend put down his cup of tea and smiled.

"It's a lovely sight," he said. "I never tire of looking at it. You know, of course, that Thonburi across the river was first a Chinese city. Then they took over Bangkok."

I had known nothing of the kind. The role of the Chinese in Siam, I said, seemed very obscure. In fact, I had hardly heard it mentioned by the Thai officials with whom I had talked. The Americans spoke in reassuring terms. For instance, they did not think that the remittances by the Chinese colony in Thailand to Communist China amounted to enough to worry about, not more than $250,000 a year, officially. Even if the unofficial total was twenty times as much, it didn't amount to anything.

"Quite true," my Chinese friend said. "The remittances are of no consequence. I suppose you have heard the Thais talk about how well the Chinese have been assimilated."

Yes, I said. That was what I had been told. Indeed, a member

42

of the Thai cabinet that very morning had explained to me that Thailand, unlike her neighbors in Southeast Asia, had no Chinese problem. He had pointed out that Indonesia had possibly 3,000,000 Chinese out of a population of 100,000,000; Malaysia had 600,000 out of 17,000,000; Burma 1,000,000 out of 28,000,000; Cambodia nearly 600,000 in 6,000,000. Singapore and Hong Kong, of course, *were* Chinese. But Thailand—well, it was a tribute to the ability of the Thais that over the centuries they had been able to live on the continent, adjacent to so powerful a neighbor without being swallowed up. True, there were probably four million Chinese in Thailand, the Thai cabinet officer said, but Thailand had maintained its independence during the terrible nineteenth century when all the rest of Asia was falling under the sway of Western Europe. She had kept out of China's hands and out of Europe's. You could be certain that whatever the threat of the twentieth century Thailand would maintain her independence. He did not know what might happen eventually in Indochina. Vietnam, he hoped, would stay free, thanks to America. But even if it fell Thailand would stand firm. Perhaps her policy might have to change. But she would keep her independence. He was not so sure that her neighbors would all be so successful. Take Burma, for instance. He was worried about Burma and even India.

My Chinese friend smiled wearily.

"I know the story very well," he said. "Now let me tell you what the situation really is."

Chinese immigrants, he said, began to come into Siam in considerable numbers between three and four hundred years ago. They came, for the most part, from South China, from Szechwan. They came with a specific and simple purpose: to acquire capital quickly and easily, to achieve in one or two generations what would be impossible or require many, many generations in China. They came to Siam, entered into business and sent their money home. In two or three generations they were able to send so much money back that their grandsons could rise to the rank of mandarins.

Chinese went to seek their fortunes in Malaysia about the same time and for the same purpose. They worked hard and saved their money. It was back-breaking labor and it took much longer. Not many Chinese in Malaysia could promote their grandsons to the mandarin rank. But many did from Siam. There was this great difference: In Siam the Chinese did not care what they did so long as they acquired gold. They cheated. They lied. They stole. Any tactic went so long as the money piled up.

The system worked well. The Chinese were good at business and commerce. The Siamese were not. The Chinese formed partnerships with the king. He granted monopolies and they shared the profits. As the Chinese grew wealthy they married Thai wives. Then they married the daughters of these unions to the Thai kings. Gradually the Thai throne grew more and more Chinese. One great Thai king took three Chinese wives. On their side the Chinese took not only Thai wives, they took Thai names. They spoke the Thai language. Within a few generations there had been such mingling that the throne was occupied by rulers who were actually Chinese—sometimes openly, sometimes under Thai names.

"It was—and is—a very assimilated country," my friend said.

The process went forward almost unimpeded until the British began to exert influence in Siam in the nineteenth century. The spirit of nationalism was growing, and for the first time the Thais became a bit sensitive about the presence of the Chinese. But still no real move against them was made until the rise of Marshal Phibun in the 1930's. Perhaps because he was himself Chinese, he embarked on an anti-Chinese policy. This continued through the Japanese occupation in World War II. Everyone thought it would end with the end of the war. But it did not. It continued to be a factor in Thai politics. But what kind of a factor was another thing. There were now five cabinet members of Chinese origin and an excellent possibility that the next Prime Minister would be a man of Chinese ancestry—Pot Saranan, the honest, rich and anti-graft Economics Development Minister.

I mentioned that Pot Saranan had told me he owned some property in the Chinese quarter of Bangkok.

"Very probably," my friend said. "You see for some years the Chinese lived there across the river. Then they moved in here and Bangkok became, to all intents and purposes, a Chinese city."

Granted this was true, I said, what bearing had it on present-day China and Thailand? What role did the Thai Chinese play in Chinese affairs?

A very great role, it seemed. The traditional system of the Thai official and the Chinese "tail" had not changed. It had only been modified. I had seen the enormous explosion of business and commerce which had hit Thailand—traffic congestion which matched that of Queens Boulevard on Long Island at rush hour; the buildings going up in every direction—two thousand new hotel rooms had been built in the last year under a law which permitted the duty-free import of construction materials and a five-year freedom from taxes to recover costs.

Where did the money come from? Much came from the enormous investment which the United States was pouring in—the great Sattahip naval base, one of the largest in the world; the huge supersonic jet bombing bases; the multilane Friendship Highway.

From these expenditures and many others there was taken from the top a percentage as the private perquisite of officials. It was not large in Thailand compared with other Asian countries—perhaps only 10 percent. In some countries the "skim" went up to 80 percent. But they were careful in Thailand. The country was, as another friend put it, "a fairly orderly conspiracy for mutual exploitation."

But this exploitation took a curious form. Thailand was a military dictatorship. Most expenditure, in one way or another, went through army hands. This was where the Chinese tail came in. The Chinese businessmen carefully watched the younger ranks of the Thai officer corps. They kept a keen eye out for men likely to rise to higher posts. When a man reached the grade of lieutenant colonel a partnership was formed. The money came from the Thai officer, the experience from the Chinese businessman. They shared the profits.

There was not a man in the upper ranks of the Thai Army who

did not have his "tail." You could see their investments everywhere. Most of the gas stations in Bangkok, for instance, were run by "tails" who had generals as partners. All over town there were signs advertising massage parlors with names like "Pretty" and "Venus." They featured "pretty girls who please you." They had twenty-four-hour telephone and liquor service. There were also twenty-four-hour "motels" and dozens of other dubious enterprises.

Perhaps there was nothing so wrong about this, but what limits were there to the business risks the "tails" might take? Suppose an opportunity arose to turn a quick profit in partnership with a Chinese businessman in Hong Kong or Singapore who was acting under orders of a principal in Red China. Would the "tail" have any scruple about engaging in this? Suppose the matter of security information was involved. After all, most of the Thai military establishment was at the service of the U.S. war effort in Vietnam. Would the Chinese "tail" have any compunction about turning over espionage data to "sweeten" a deal with a Chinese Communist partner?

And what, after all, were the political sympathies of the Chinese tails? To be sure, they had pictures of Chiang Kai-shek in their offices. But, my Chinese friend said, he knew these men intimately. He visited their homes as well as their establishments. There weren't many who did not have a picture of Mao Tse-tung conveniently available—just in case.

The Thais were confident of their ability to stay clear of China's power, even if the United States pulled out of Vietnam. But where would the influence of the hidden Chinese minority be thrown in such an event? Would the Thais actually be masters in their own household? Were they masters at this moment?

"To me," the Chinese said, "this talk of assimilation is really just a matter of sweeping things under a rug. The Chinese are here. They are everywhere. They are merely somewhat invisible. But they are still Chinese, and, mark my word, most of them, whatever they may feel about Mao and the Communists, are proud that

China is now standing on her own feet and making the world respect her strength. I know how they feel. I feel a bit like that myself."

I could find no one who thought that the Thais would veer from their all-out commitment to the American side of the Vietnam war, although for propaganda purposes they constantly minimized this dedication.

Pot Saranan insisted that he would not permit the Americans to pour so much money into Thailand that the country's economy was knocked off its rails. He said they kept the example of Vietnam firmly in mind. Nothing like that would be permitted to happen in Thailand. Just that week he had refused a $30 million American loan and turned to the World Bank instead.

Yet Thais and foreigners agreed that inflation was on the rise. With the steady influx of American personnel (probably pushing fifty thousand by early 1967), there was a rising tide of complaint, particularly about prostitution, bars, crime and huge price increases in the vicinity of the American air complexes.

"Of course," one American said, "they complain. I don't blame them. On the other hand, when a peasant finds his daughter can earn five times as much on a mattress in Bangkok in a day than she can in two years on a farm—well . . . "

On the great question of Thailand's future, no Thailander had more confidence than Thanat Khoman, the Thai Foreign Minister, a vigorous, talkative, frank man whose star had risen remarkably.

It was Thanat whose behind-the-scenes maneuvering opened the way for Indonesia and Malaysia to end their "confrontation" after the unhappy downfall of President Sukarno. It was Thanat who launched the nine-member ASPAC all-Asian grouping with the Seoul conference. And it was Thanat who proposed that Asia and Asia alone take on the task of resolving the Vietnam war through an all-Asia conference.

On a continent where neither statesmanship nor leadership had been highly visible Thanat was outstanding.

I found him a blunt and forceful supporter of U.S. policy in

Vietnam. It had already won, he was convinced. He saw the contest as a straight-out competition with the Chinese, and he wrote the Chinese off as losers. Not only in Vietnam but all over Asia. The tide, he believed, began to turn in 1965 and had mounted steadily. He cited the downfall of Sukarno as the greatest setback, followed by the end of confrontation, the break between Peking and Moscow, the loss of China's footholds in Africa. The Chinese leadership struggle of 1966 to him was merely another evidence of the crisis in China policy.

"I don't understand the Americans," he said. "We must take the long view. The reason we Thais are on the U.S. side is because we have confidence in U.S. victory. China is losing—all along the line."

Thanat had sharp words for men like Senators Fulbright and Mansfield and the critics of President Johnson. Their criticism, he felt sure, was simply encouraging the North Vietnamese and the Vietcong to hang on. "They should register as foreign agents," he said. "We must have more confidence in our policy because it is winning."

But while he believed China was the main opponent in Asia he did not believe she had started the Vietnamese war. That, in his view, was the simple product of a desire by North Vietnam to dominate all Vietnam. Nor did he think the Chinese had started the Korean War. They were pushed into that by Russia. China, he felt, had no desire to fight the United States. Not now. In ten or fifteen years, however, things might be different.

Did he think that Thailand could maintain her independence in event of an American pull-out from Vietnam? Absolutely. Would her policy change? Ah, that was another question.

I sought out an American who had spent most of his adult life in Siam. He knew the country before World War II, spent some time in the remarkable American OSS group which operated behind the Japanese lines in Siam and had seen a good deal of postwar Thailand.

He had great respect for the Thais. He felt they had made a remarkable record in Asia. But he also believed they exaggerated their ability to maintain an independent course in the face of great pressures.

"It is true that they did not become a colony when all of Asia was going under," he said. "And they stayed out of Chinese hands. But how did they do it? They are a good deal more Chinese than they realize. And there are those who will say that the Chinese actually took them over. They kept out of the clutches of the French and the British largely because they could play the two powers against each other."

He felt that the Thais were running risks in two directions. The first arose from the size of the military establishment which the Americans were putting into Thailand.

This was of a weight which seemed likely to match the facilities built in South Vietnam. Its heart was the complex of six great air bases, including two equipped to handle the supersonic B-52's of the U.S. Strategic Air Force. One of these bases was the Don Muang air base at Bangkok. The other was the enormous Sattahip base with its 11,500-foot runways. Adjacent to it was the Sattahip naval base, probably the largest in the Far East if completed according to plans. And linking all these installations were pipelines, fuel dumps and the broad concrete strip of Friendship Highway—an arrow pointed straight at the corner where Laos, Thailand and Vietnam met.

All of this had been built in official secrecy—a secrecy which had no real existence since every installation had been extensively described and written about in the world press. The secrecy lay only in the reticence whereby neither Americans nor Thais officially spoke of the presence of Americans in Thailand—15,000 at the beginning of 1966, 35,000 by autumn, 1966—how many before 1967 reached its conclusion?

What was the purpose of these massive constructions? Was it, as the Americans officially (but privately) insisted, just for the purpose of prosecuting the Vietnam war and helping Thailand "protect

§   49

herself" against a Communist menace which, for practical purposes, did not exist? Or was it, as some speculated, part of an American build-up for the coming war against China? Were these the bases from which the Strategic Air Force hoped to make its strike against the Chinese nuclear installations? They were far closer to Lanchow and Paotow than Guam. The Strategic Air Force, for reasons of tact—and violent Japanese protest—was not using its Okinawa bases for operations in Southeast Asia. Nor would it probably use Okinawa against China when, as and if the signal was given.

For many reasons Thailand seemed from the Strategic Air Force viewpoint to be an ideal base against China. It was neutral. It was wholly committed to the United States. It was a big, stable country with much room for facilities. It had a strong military regime which was not likely to make trouble whatever the United States did. It was located a long, long way from the bases of Chinese land power yet within easy striking distance of the principal targets for the big U.S. bombers.

No Americans of official status would give the slightest support to such ideas. But there were Air Force men who conceded that "if worst came to worst" Thailand would be very useful.

There was not the slightest sign that this prospect—if it existed—bothered the Thais. They were firm in their attitude that whatever happened they would be able to come through with flying colors. I did not think it likely that the Thais had ever seriously contemplated the consequences of involving their country in nuclear warfare.

Yet if American nuclear bombing was carried out from Thai bases against China and this provoked reaction by the Chinese or by the Russians, could the Thais expect their country to escape?

The other risk which Thailand faced was that the United States might be driven from South Vietnam. Or might abandon it in disgust (and there were not a few Asians in the summer of 1966, I found, who thought this might ultimately happen).

What then? Would Thailand become a fall-back position for the Americans? Would the United States utilize its powerful air and naval network in Thailand to hold back the Communist tide?

On this question the Thais were very firm. They would not provide a fall-back position. If the Americans left Vietnam they would not be able to retreat to Thailand.

But the Thais were equally strong in their conviction that Thailand would not topple like a domino. Indeed, I found no one, American, non-American or Thai, who thought the domino theory applied to Thailand. In general, the domino theory seemed to be more popular in Washington, D.C., than in Asia.

Even if Vietnam went Communist, the Thais felt they could hold the line against a Communist takeover. After all, they said, they had no real Communist problem. This was true. However, some Americans believed the Thais were courting eventual trouble in their northeast triangle, where more than one-third of the country's population (many of them *montagnards*, non-Thai minorities and some refugees from North Vietnam) lived in conditions close to chronic starvation. There were about ten million people in the area. They got virtually no economic aid from the central government. Indeed, central government authority was only lightly exerted in the region. To the Thai official it was Siberia. He would rather do anything than go there.

But these conditions constituted social dynamite. One worried American told me he had organized a trip for a group of Bangkok officials to Vietnam to demonstrate to them what had happened in that country where similar social inequities were allowed to fester. He wanted them to see the kinds of programs which were required to lift the living standards of the people from the starvation level.

The Thai northeast could become a crisis area if Communist influence in Southeast Asia were to grow.

"But," said probably the best-informed American in the country, "I'd bet on the Thais to come through. Of course, they would kick us out. It is silly to talk about Thailand as a fall-back position. If we leave Vietnam we will be packing our bags in Thailand soon after."

"The truth of the matter is," said a shrewd Englishman, "these countries have lived together in Asia a lot longer than we have. Maybe they will go on living together a lot longer in the future—without us."

There really was no way of proving the soundness of a remark like that. But one morning Charlotte and I took a boat at the landing stage beside the Oriental Hotel. We went up the river and presently were threading through the maze of canals which give to Bangkok a quality which no other city in the Orient possesses. We found ourselves in a kind of Eastern Venice in which the canals or *klongs*, as they are called, replaced the streets and water lapped at the doorstep of every house. Here was a barbershop, its clients arriving one by one in their little boats. Here a grocery store, the day's customers beginning to crowd the narrow canal. Here a smart young woman whose gown may have come from the Rue Saint-Honoré paddled her narrow dugout. There three children dove in the slimy water. Beyond them a mother knelt on the lowest step, put a package of Fab beside her and began the day's laundry.

There were big cement barges, propelled by motors; sleek taxis with outboard motors suspended from a rod in the rear; a soot-smudged family poled a coal boat through the canal; another slowly headed a heavy scow of timbers into the traffic.

Here there was a wider canal and a dense congestion of vegetable and fruit boats, there a landing that led up to a great golden temple to Buddha.

Our way led deeper and deeper into the crisscross of *klongs*. Now we were so far from the western city that it was hard to believe one existed. This was Bangkok. This was the heart of the Siamese city—as it had been for generations, the Siamese life unchanged and unchanging. Here, I thought, was the reason for the confidence of the Thais in their ability to maintain their integrity, their independence, in the face of whatever threat—be it Chinese domination or the suffocating rain of American gold. Here was their life being lived as it had been for centuries. It had a tough, sinewy quality of its own. The Siamese had learned that to survive in Asia you must be supple and patient, you must bend now this way, now that way. But, above all, you must hold on to your own, your own way of life, your own customs, your own gods. I did not think that this lesson, well learned, would quickly slip from Siamese minds. Whatever happened there would be a Siam for a good many centuries. Siam would exist in Asia as an Asian country regardless of what Peking did or what Washington did. So long as no nuclear bombs were dropped Siam would go on.

5

To the Faery Station

A BURLY AMERICAN WAS SPRAWLED ACROSS THE WORN LEATHER SEAT of the compartment when I boarded the Bangkok train for Vientiane. He wore a light blue sport shirt, open at the neck, and looked up dully when I came in.

"I hate to tell you this," he said as I glanced from the seat to the upper berth. "You're upstairs."

It was not a pleasant prospect. The temperature was over 90 and humid. I had been told that the train was clean, the ride pleasant and comfortable. It looked as though the information was wrong. I began to wonder what I was doing, taking an Asian train from one remote capital to another even more remote; whether there would be anything in Laos to justify the heat and discomfort of an overnight tropical train.

My companion offered little to raise my spirits. He was, he informed me, a pilot for Air America. He'd come from Vientiane to Bangkok for his daughter's graduation from high school. "It's the sorta thing you gotta do," he said. "Kids expect it."

But he was not happy. Ordinarily he could deadhead down to Bangkok on an Air America plane. But for some incomprehensible reason orders had been issued: no more deadheading. If he wanted to go to Bangkok he had to fly commercial—Thai airlines or Royal Laotian and pay his way. A lousy deal. The only thing worse was the train. He had a pilot's aversion to trains. In fact, I wondered if he had ever ridden one before. Apparently he had taken it to save a few dollars. The ride would be awful, he announced, and in the morning did I know what to expect? The train didn't even go to Vientiane. It stopped at Nongkhai. You had to take a pedicab, go through customs, then a ferry across the river and on into Vientiane. Be lucky to get there before lunchtime.

The train pulled out of the station, and we moved smoothly through the endless expanse of Bangkok suburbia. Was there a restaurant car on the train? I asked. He gave me a withering glance. There was—if you could take that Thai food. For himself, he had brought a chocolate bar and a box of Nabiscos.

He put his chin on his hand and stared glumly out the window. It looked like a long trip. A very long trip. My companion informed me that he was considering giving the whole thing up and quitting Laos. Sure, he had a contract. So what? The life was too hard. The flying, of course, was terrible. I had no idea what it was like up there. What did he do? A cagey smile came over his face. He flew "to the north." On lots of things. It was not so bad when the monsoon came. But during the dry season it was awful. The gooks—his word for natives—burned the forest then. It was always burning. Smoke all over. Filled the valleys. Between the smoke and the mist you never knew where you were. That was bad. The worst was being separated from the family. They were in Bangkok. The little woman liked it better there and the school for the kids—two girls, ten and fourteen—was a lot better. They had looked at the school in Vientiane. Well, lots of the fellows had their kids in it. But it just wasn't suitable. Not for American kids. After all, they had come from Sarasota. Great town, Sarasota. Good schools. Great place for kids. He got down to Bangkok at least once a month to see his family. But now, if they couldn't even use their own planes . . . That was too much.

I sympathized and set out, despite his warning, to investigate the restaurant car. It was clean and airy. The waiter was pleasant, the menu decent, the food appetizing. I ran into an American sergeant. He was a Special Forces man who had come to Thailand a couple of months earlier to train Thai troops. Before that he had been in Vietnam. He was a little sore about coming to Thailand so soon. He was based in Okinawa and he was fearful that by some process of military arithmetic his service in Vietnam and Thailand would not be counted as combat and he might have to do another tour. That he had no desire for, but he liked Thailand and Thai troops.

"They're better than those Viets," he said. "Believe me, I never would have turned my back on the Viets. No telling what they'd do. But these fellows—I'd go anywhere with them."

He was stationed at a big American air base. He had learned Vietnamese, or so he said, in an army crash program, studying three hours a day. Now he was learning Thai. He had been at it six weeks and found it easy. I didn't test his knowledge.

When I got back to the compartment I found my friend from Sarasota turned in for the night. Somewhat apprehensive, I clambered up to the upper bunk. The window was wide open, the ceiling fan swung gently, and to my surprise I found the upper as pleasant and cool as the lower was humid and close. Before the night was over I had to draw the wool blanket up to my chin. I sneaked a glance at the unhappy flying man. He was sprawled in his shorts, his face red, breathing heavily and sweating. "I hate to tell you this," I whispered, "but you're downstairs." He stirred lightly but did not awaken.

The pilot was one of scores of Air America pilots, I was to learn later, carrying out missions in Laos. There were two large on-the-record U.S. air operations in Laos. One was Air America, a subsidiary-of-record of the CIA, and the other a contract operation for which Continental Airlines, it was said, was receiving at least $10 million. The pilots signed contracts for two or three years at $3,000 a month.

The operations were described as being in support of the U.S. AID mission. The pilots flew C-123's, C-43's and C-46's. They also flew helicopters and special single-engined Swiss planes, designed for mountain operations. It was no picnic. Half the mountain people in Laos delighted in taking pot shots at the planes and the losses were considerable. No one seemed to know exactly what the planes and pilots were up to. They dropped radio sets and radar equipment. They dropped mysterious bags and cartons which, some said, contained arms, munitions and, possibly, French piasters—of the issues prior to 1901, weighing 27 grams in silver. To whom were the drops made? Presumably to "friendlys." This was the current military jargon for little clusters of "friendly" natives who were supposed to constitute islands of strength in a dubious and confused situation like Laos. One group of friendlys was the Meo tribe, a tribe which was to be found only on mountainsides at the level of 3,000 to 3,500 feet. These people were extremely fond of French piasters—of the issues prior to 1901. They melted down the silver or sewed the piasters into their clothing. They used the silver to decorate the muzzles of the flintlocks which they made for themselves and they used it for pipe decorations, bracelets, necklaces, headwear, dowries, whip handles and dagger shafts.

The Meos were on excellent terms with U.S. AID. They were independent hillsmen. Unlike some of their compatriots they did not sell their girls as slaves or prostitutes. And they were very wealthy. The wealth came from opium. Other drops were made to Yao tribesmen. The Yaos lived on hilltops above the four-thousand-foot level. There was a big Yao program—all very mysterious.

I woke early in the cool morning. I had been told that the scenery in northern Thailand would be spectacular. It wasn't. Just open hilly country, occasional cultivated areas and jungles.

Young Tammy Arbuckle, a tousle-haired Scots lad, met me at the Nongkhai station. There was no trouble. In a minute we had a pedicab and soon had passed through customs and were crossing the wide Mekong in a launch to a landing stage on the Laotian side which a sign proclaimed to be the "Faery Station."

We drove into Vientiane. I was shown the Premier's residence and the Foreign Office, just back from the dusty flats of the Mekong River. A company of dirty troops, their guns tumbled in a heap beside a column of jeeps, was lolling in a side street beside the Foreign Office.

"Gosh," said Tammy, "I wonder if there's going to be a coup."

It was not exactly idle wonder. Vientiane, as usual, was in the throes of a crisis. General Thao Ma, commander of the Air Force, was defying orders of Premier Souvanna Phouma to return to Vientiane and submit to the government. He refused to leave his headquarters in the south at Suvannaket and was sending his planes out almost every day to attack the Ho Chi Minh Trail. He was also flying foreign correspondents down to the Cambodian frontier, where, he insisted, he had discovered a "Prince Sihanouk trail" which led up from the Mekong River at Stungtreng, along Route Nationale No. 13 for forty miles, across the Se Khong at Siempang, then up along the banks of the Se Khong to the Laos border near Hat Hai and a junction with the Ho Chi Minh Trail. He was calling for permission to extend his bombing operations to Cambodia and (as far as anyone really knew) might already be engaged in this rather spectacular task.

General Thao Ma, a man of Vietnamese blood, presented a problem to the Premier, whose sworn policy was neutrality—although neutrality of a peculiarly Laotian variety. It was strongly suspected that General Thao was not really acting entirely on his own. He was known to have some close U.S. Air Force advisers, and there was a suspicion that his belligerence might be part of a campaign by some not too easily identifiable Americans who were itching to extend the war to northern Cambodia and southern Laos. These elusive Americans, it was said, wanted to put several divisions of ground troops into the area to cut right across Laos and Cambodia and thus halt supplies which they imagined were getting through to the Vietcong and the North Vietnamese.

Premier Souvanna Phouma might not have objected too much to General Thao's private war against Cambodia except that Thao refused to use his planes against the Pathet Lao, the home-grown Laotian Communist movement which controlled at least one-third (some thought possibly one-half) of his kingdom.

Thus the Premier was trying to get General Thao to come back to Vientiane and put the air force under the government's command. The General was refusing. He said he would come to Vientiane only if he was given a guarantee of his personal safety by the Premier, the Finance Minister (one of the few generally recognized honest men in Laotian politics) and, most important of all, U.S. Ambassador William Sullivan.

General Thao's demand was no irresponsible quirk. Only too vividly in his recollection was the fate of a predecessor who had yielded to government entreaty to come to Vientiane for a "conference" and had been machine-gunned to death in his house two days after arrival.

The quarrel between General Thao and the Government simmered all summer long and finally in October came to a climax when the General sent eight of his B-28 bombers to attack the Government military headquarters just outside Vientiane. The Americans tried to halt him at the last minute but failed and more than 30 Laotians were killed. However, the coup d'etat did not succeed and the General fled with a handful of supporters across the frontier into Thailand. The Thais gave him refuge but agreed to send the bombers back to Laos.

Vientiane, I found, was not a capital where anyone relied on anyone's word. Just around the corner from the government offices, in the very center of town, stood a good-sized stone house, heavily surrounded by barbed-wire entanglements. At the corners there were sandbagged machine-gun posts and on the walls were floodlights for use at night. This was the Pathet Lao headquarters, and within a picked guard of 150 troops was stationed to defend it against assault, a sensible precaution it seemed to me, since the Souvanna Phouma government was exerting every effort to exterminate the Pathet Lao. The presence of the Pathet headquarters in Vientiane was tangible evidence of Laotian "neutrality." Souvanna Phouma's government was made up of representatives of the right, of the center and of the left—the Pathet Lao. While the Pathet Lao did not play any role in the government, their headquarters was witness that the principle of neutrality, however warped, was still observed, at least in the breach.

There was about Laos a bemused quality. It was difficult to think of it as a country. It seemed rather more like the invention of some faintly plausible Hollywood script writer. One thing seemed clear. It was not a nation despite its recognition as such by the world powers, despite its membership in the United Nations, despite its Prime Minister, and its pleasant King, Savang Vathana (who had just returned from an extended tour of the Soviet Union in the company of Prince Souvanna Phouma). And, in actual truth, there never really had been any country named Laos—not since a brief interlude that ended in the seventeenth century. Then Laos split into three kingdoms, and since those medieval times it had lost whatever semblance of unity it may have possessed. Part of it fell into Siamese hands, part was taken over by the French, part simply dropped back into control of the regional tribes. Even the idea of Laotian nationality was a fuzzy one. About half the population was Laotian. But the rest was splintered into diverse groups, most of whom had been at war with each other for centuries. And more Laotians lived in Thailand than in Laos.

Of all the states of Southeast Asia none, it seemed to me, could be more intimately concerned with the outcome in Vietnam, with the rise of Chinese power, with the American presence in Southeast Asia. The whole of Laos's eastern frontier bordered on Vietnam and was directly involved in the war. On the north Laos shared a border with China—a remote and mountainous one. What went on there? Vientiane could not have been more indifferent. The border area was controlled by a local war lord in firm alliance with the Pathet Lao. The war lord's relations with the Chinese were so cozy the

Chinese had built two highways into the area to facilitate trade. There was no sign of any southward push by the Chinese. But they were positioned strategically for a thrust any time they desired.

The relationship of the Chinese with the Pathet Lao was equally cozy. There was, of course, a Chinese Embassy in Vientiane. There was also an embassy at Pathet Lao headquarters in Xiengkhouang, near the Plain of Jarres. It was not called an embassy, of course. It was called a trade and cultural mission. There was said to be a company of Chinese troops to protect it. The Laotian Government had protested the presence of the Chinese a year ago. The Chinese said they would do something. But nothing had happened.

Nor was there any sign of Laotian interest in China itself. The Laotian mission in Peking was left in the hands of a second secretary who never responded to telegrams from the Foreign Office. Vientiane had to send a message through the Indians to see if the man was still there. He had not sent one report since being assigned to Peking. No first-rank Laotian diplomat would think of going to Peking—it was regarded as worse than exile. The only man in the Laotian Foreign Office who knew anything about China was assigned to other duties.

China seemed very distant to the Laotians. It was as though it were another planet, or something glimpsed in a dream.

And this had a basis in fact. For the reality in Laos was not China, not Vietnam. It was opium.

I had first heard about the opium in Bangkok. An intelligence officer explained the problem as he saw it—or as he wanted me to see it. There was in the remote and rugged corner where the Laotian, Thai, Burmese and Chinese frontiers came together a quadrangle of possibly 250,000 square miles where none of the governments had real jurisdiction. This was Poppy-land. Here for decades the hill farmers had raised poppy for the opium trade. And here they still did.

Many eager hands had a part in this traffic. There were, for instance, the Kuomintang troops whose relations ostensibly had long since been severed with Formosa. These were the troops who fell back through Yünnan in the last fighting against the Communists in 1949. They had taken up positions on the frontier in remote areas of Burma and Thailand. Later, in a mysterious and never fully revealed operation, the Chinese Nationalists and the CIA had flown more Chinese troops and arms and munitions into the area. They were, under the command of General Tuan Shi Wen, ostensibly to conduct forays into Communist China and to gather intelligence. And in fact they held control of the wild area, together with the Shan tribesmen, their loyal and energetic allies.

How many Chinese had been originally involved in this was never quite certain. Possibly twenty or thirty thousand at the peak. Not unnaturally, the operation aroused violent protests from the Burmese. They complained to the United States, and the CIA was compelled to disavow its role in the operation and ostensibly sever all connections with the Chinese. The Burmese sent government troops to the north and gradually drove the Chinese back into a tight corner adjacent to Thailand.

Now, my Bangkok informant told me, the Chinese had gotten out of Burma entirely and were positioned in northwest Thailand. They had set themselves up in fine modern barracks. They were protected by perimeter defenses and light mountain artillery. They had planes, landing strips and heliports. Woe betide anyone who ventured into their area without their permission. When, for instance, U.S. AID parties had missions in that part of Thailand, they regularly passed word to the Chinese garrisons.

What, I asked, are the Chinese doing there?

The opium business, my friend replied. They don't pay much attention to anything else. But they are very much concerned with opium.

Later on, in Burma, I was to find that the picture was not exactly as described in Bangkok. Far from having gotten out of Burma, there were still about five thousand Chinese there, according to Burmese estimates. About two thousand of them, the Burmese said, had been more or less assimilated in the hill villages. The others were in the opium business.

The KMT troops, as they were universally called, were the major transporters and organizers of the raw opium trade. The poppy itself was grown largely by Shan tribesmen who lived in all four of the countries involved. It was purely accidental whether they happened to grow their opium in Communist China or highly anti-Communist Thailand. This was the source of the flamboyant stories of Chinese Communist participation in the opium business. Certainly, the Chinese Communists were aware of what went on. But no one seemed to believe the Chinese Communists got a direct share in the profits. It was true, however, that they showed little interest in disturbing the Shan tribesmen or curtailing their role in the opium traffic. The Shans, by Chinese law, were permitted to go back and forth across the Chinese frontier without interference so long as they lived within fifty miles of the boundary.

It seemed to me that the Chinese Communists might well have an interest in the opium traffic quite similar to that of the CIA. Although there was evidence of CIA links to all the participants in the trade, I did not believe the CIA was a direct partner. However, it was an indirect beneficiary. Its interest was in intelligence and possibly in clandestine operations in China. The opium trade financed the livelihood of a strange and diverse assortment of groups, most of whom had links into Communist China and most of whom were used in one way or another and at one time or another by the CIA. This was certainly true of the Shan tribes. It was certainly true of the so-called KMT troops. It was likely to be true of the Meo and the Yao. Did the Communist Chinese make use of the same tribes for much the same purposes? It would not be surprising.

I had heard that at one time the CIA had contemplated "preclusive buying" of opium—the buying up of the whole output in order to monopolize control of the illicit trade. I had also heard that the CIA was turning over relations with the hill tribes to the

U.S. AID people, with the idea of trying to find some other cash crop which the farmers could grow in the remote hills. The Burmese, I learned, were also trying to find some crop that could be as attractive to the hillsmen as the poppy. But since AID, in Laos at any rate, seemed to be one of the favorite covers for the CIA, I wondered if this wasn't just letting the left hand take over something of which the right hand was a little weary.

It was not merely a matter of finding another profitable crop. The farmers did not make more than a subsistence living from cultivation of the poppy. But the growing of the poppy had acquired a kind of cultural and superstitious significance. It did not seem likely that AID teams would find it easy to get the hill people to abandon a traditional way of life.

The role of the KMT in the opium traffic was important. They possessed the organizing skill and the resources to handle the supply in large quantities. Harvesting was done in the traditional way. When the poppy seed pod was ripe it was nicked with a knife. The raw opium oozed out and solidified. This was scraped off by hand with a knife, then rolled into large balls, which in turn were packed in jute sacks. The tribesmen, under KMT supervision, made up armed caravans, using as many as 150 men to guard a pack train, and brought the opium down by muleback to assembly points where it was picked up by the KMT copters and planes. The KMT flew the opium to secret transfer points where it was turned over in its brown form to other transporters.

There were many hands in this business. Did any of the American pilots in Laos participate? This would be difficult to prove, but Laos was the favorite corridor for the traffic and many planes and pilots were available. It was a familiar route. It was not involved in the war in Vietnam directly (direct flights from northern Thailand and Laos to Saigon had been suspended after the loss of several planes over war zones). Laos had another advantage. Opium was not illegal in Laos. It was a legitimate article of commerce. It could be openly smoked. Indeed, the opium den was a familiar feature of the Vientiane landscape. Some establishments in Vientiane had recently been closed after a succession of scandals. But you could still smoke at dens on Vientiane's strip. Cheap, too. Only 60, 70, or 80 kips a pipe.

Opium was a major factor in the Laotian economy—possibly *the* major factor. As Finance Minister Sisouk Na Champassak told me, gold and opium were the principal preoccupations of Vientiane when he took office in 1964. He did not pretend that the situation had changed too much. The largest source of Laotian revenue was the transit traffic in gold. It came into Vientiane at the rate of three, four and five tons a month—but never stayed. The Laotian revenues derived from the transit fees. Why should such enormous quantities of gold come to so remote and isolated an Asian capital? Champassak shrugged his shoulders. "Who knows? There must be profit in it for someone."

There was, indeed.

"You should be at the airport sometime when the planes come in from Saigon," a friend said. "And you should watch those beautiful Vietnamese ladies get off the planes, their bodies clanking and swaying from the weight of the gold bars taped around their middles."

Vientiane is one of the world's free gold markets. You can buy and sell gold there, any quantity for any purpose from anywhere, no questions asked.

"Suppose," a banker said, "you have acquired some diamonds in Hong Kong. Let's not worry about where they came from. You take them to Saigon. There you sell them for gold bars. You bring the gold to Vientiane. You sell it to a man who smuggles it into India. The Indians absorb millions of dollars in gold bars every year. What do you do with the profits? Perhaps you invest them in heroin and ship that to Hong Kong and the process goes around again."

There are so many variations of the trade that it is impossible even to imagine them all. But one thing is certain. The gold flows to and through Vientiane because somebody makes a profit in it.

But what about the raw opium? Once it gets to Laos it undergoes refinement. It used to be refined to brown opium or what is known in the trade as "morphine base." But with the Vietnam war and the dangers of losing shipments heroin is easier to handle. There have been opened in Laos in the last year or so at least two heroin-refining plants. The locations are no secret. One is just outside the royal capital of Luang Prabang. The other is in Sayaboury on the west bank of the Mekong.

For one reason or another there seemed to be an affinity between the military and the opium trade. It began with the KMT troops. In Laos there were open charges of a link between high army officers and a very active right-wing army family and the dope business. These elements had their connections with important figures in the Thai Army.

Refined into morphine base or heroin, the product was moved down through Laos and Thailand to Bangkok, to Saigon, to Singapore, to Hong Kong, to Taiwan, to Tokyo—and beyond, to the U.S.A. This was easy in the era of an enormous American presence in the Far East. There were so many planes flying in so many directions, so many troops moving here and there, such a bustle of traffic, the problem was really no problem at all once you figured out a way to avoid having your courier planes shot down over the Viet battlefields.

This, it seemed evident, was what Laos was really about. Not the war. Not China. Not her dubious neutrality.

On a hot afternoon I went out to the Vientiane airport. The sun beat down in a dazzle. Inside the airport there was a noisy hubbub in the big second-floor lounge. A table had been set up in the middle of the room near the bar and a beefy American was pulling some Piper-Heidsieck bottles from a PX shopping bag. He untwisted the wire from a cork, aimed the bottle in the direction of a pretty dark-haired Laotian girl at the bar, and let it go. The cork hit the ceiling and the crowd cheered.

"It's a going-away part for some U.S. AID personnel," a friend told me.

I looked over at the American group. Most of them seemed to be jowly characters with bright sport shirts, dark glasses and wives whose Thai silk dresses were stretched tight across the shoulders and hips. With them were a number of Asians, not Laotians.

"Those are TCN," my friend said. "That means Third Country Nationals."

AID, it seemed, hired large numbers of TCN's to "deal" with the Laotians, to carry out supervisory and clerical chores. This left the American personnel free to relax from the tropical sun, to shop every day in the big PX which they had established in the U.S. AID ghetto about four miles outside town.

The U.S. AID people said they could not find competent Laotians to do the work and they had to import foreigners, mostly from the Philippines and Korea. This was not popular with the Laotians, who said there was no way for the Americans to have any idea of Laotian reactions to American programs since everything was filtered through third parties not all of whom could be trusted to give honest accounts, verbal or arithmetical.

In another corner of the lounge there was a second group, another farewell party. The pretty Eurasian mistress of a crew-cut American pilot whose middle had noticeably thickened was going off to Bangkok. Around her neck swung a garland of gold spangles. She wore a golden belt and with her was a poodle in a large wickerware carrier.

The pilot worked either for Continental or Air America. The handsome young woman heading for Bangkok was what is known in Vientiane as a "professional mistress." She earned about $400 a month. Not bad pay, but she loved to gamble and she had little left at the end of the month. A member of the farewell party was a Brooklyn Irishman. He had been flying in Vientiane for three years. His mistress was now getting $600 a month, the gossips said, even though she had given the Irishman a case of syphilis.

There was a wait for the Bangkok plane. At the far side of the field five chubby A-28 bombers took off, one by one, like buzzing bees.

"Going out for the late afternoon bombing," my friend said. He did not say what they would be bombing. It might be the Pathet Lao. It might be the Ho Chi Minh Trail. Or it might be targets in North Vietnam.

I paused to look out the window. My attention was attracted to an old DC-3, painted rather a gaudy green and bearing an exotic name painted in Laotian. "What kind of an airline is that?" I asked in wonder.

My friend laughed. "Remember what I've been telling you? Well, there it is: Air Opium."

The line, it appeared, flew the Luang Prabang–Vientiane run. Not many passengers, but lots of freight.

Finally, the Bangkok plane was called. We walked slowly out on the field. Down toward the end, gleaming in the sunshine, I saw three all-white helicopters bearing the initials CIC—Commission Internationale Contrôle. There they were, the symbol of Laotian neutrality, pure and white and glistening, symbol of the world's interest in Laos, evidence of the reality of the Geneva Accords, which guaranteed the sovereignty of Laos, which pledged the great powers of the world to maintain a free and independent Laos, safe from war, safe from aggression.

I boarded the plane for Bangkok and we taxied slowly past the three white helicopters. Safe from war? Neutral? Secure from aggression? By China or the U.S.A.? A sovereign nation? I sorely doubted it. Safe from opium? Not a chance. The most realistic thing I'd seen in all Laos, or so it now seemed to me, had been the sign beside the river bank which read: "Faery Station." Faery Station—gateway to a kingdom not even a fairy tale could make credible.

6

Asia's Cromwell

WE WERE FOLLOWING THE IRRAWADDY COMING SOUTH FROM PAGAN, and the country was spread out below us, open and wide and as much like desert as Arizona. The pilot of the plane—it was General Ne Win's personal C-47, especially fitted out just the year before in Hong Kong, with gray walls of plastic brocade, blue upholstered seats, magenta-and-black curtains at the windows—called me to the cockpit. He wanted to show me the terrain because it was here, flying a fighter-bomber, low over a road jammed with transport, that he had personally destroyed a column of Karens marching on Rangoon in the desperate fighting of 1948–49 when the Burmese Goverment tottered in the balance.

The Captain had won the DSM in that action. He didn't call his enemies Karens, in describing the fighting; he called them Communists. He was a fine flying officer, and when he was not piloting General Ne Win's plane he was heading up a squadron of the fighter force. He had fought through all the struggles which Burma had undergone since World War II, and his opponents, whether they were Karen or Kachin or Shan, he lumped together as Communists. He thought that he had had about as much experience as any man in the world in fighting Communists, and he thought that his leader, General Ne Win, probably was better at it than anyone else.

69

As we flew south over the red-brown Burmese earth he talked about the war in Vietnam. He was worried about the war and he was worried about the United States. He felt very close to Americans. He had gotten his higher training at the Command School at Maxwell Field and he had flown all over the United States with his American Air Force buddies. He knew Las Vegas and Los Angeles, New York and Boston. He had seen the French Quarter in New Orleans and had stayed at the Shamrock in Houston. He spoke English like an American and his eyes glistened at the thought of going back to the United States. But he was not happy about Vietnam.

"We know how to handle Communists," he said. "You must fight them and fight them hard. You must hurt them so badly that they don't want to fight any more. But you can't simply go out and kill, kill, kill. That's not enough."

You had to have a faith, he said, you had to have a faith and a belief in something that was more powerful than the Communist belief, and when the time came and they were tired of fighting you had to sit with them and show them that your faith was stronger than theirs and that it was better for them to stop fighting and learn to accept your faith.

"We have Buddhism," he said. "And it is stronger than Communism. Of course, if there are some who won't stop fighting, there is just one answer. Kill them."

He was despondent about Vietnam. The Americans, he said, had already lost there. They had lost because they did not understand that the white man could no longer fight in Asia and win. It didn't make any difference who he was or where he was fighting—or what for. Asia would not permit a white man to win a war on her continent. Not any longer.

The United States did not seem to perceive this. The war in Vietnam could have been won if we had been willing to let the Vietnamese fight it. When we took it over ourselves, we doomed ourselves to defeat. This depressed him very much. Because in the end it would be a victory for the Communists—for the Chinese. And he was dedicated to the cause of fighting not only the Communists but the Chinese.

The voice was that of a Burmese Air Force commander, speaking with just a trace of the Southern accent he acquired at Maxwell Field. But the sentiments were not unfamiliar to me. I had heard something similar from an Englishman in Bangkok who had lived most of his life in the Orient. He, too, was a man very friendly to the American cause, a man who felt that the danger from the Chinese was urgent. But he was not happy about Vietnam.

"You are putting too much in there," he said. "And there is danger you will do the same here, in Thailand. You must not tip the balance and make it a white man's war against Asians. That won't go down any more. You just turn the tide against yourselves and give the other fellow a lift."

Moreover, he warned, as American troops took more and more of the burden of the war on their backs, the Vietnamese would relax and opt out of the fighting.

"You can already see it happening," he said. "Why not? If Americans are willing to do the fighting, why should the Vietnamese worry? That's just human psychology at work."

The Burmese Air Force man spoke for himself. But he spoke in terms I was to hear from many Burmese military men—and from General Ne Win. It was not difficult to talk to the military in Burma. In fact, it was difficult to talk to anyone else, for one of the characteristics of General Ne Win's government was that every member of his cabinet, except for the Foreign Minister, and almost every other high official was an army man. It was an unusual combination. The officers were unusual, particularly for Asia. Like their chief they seemed to be bone-honest. There are almost as many kinds of government in Asia as there are countries. But honesty in government is another thing. It is to be found in Burma, but I don't know where else.

Burma had not been on our itinerary. Burma was a vital region on China's periphery, but for more than three years—since General Ne Win took control—it had been sealed to foreigners. Diplomatic missions had been sharply reduced, most foreign aid had been discontinued, newspapermen were banned, the tourist trade was halted and even businessmen could not get visas. Burma was by way of turning into a hermit country. Even China was more accessible.

The draconian measures undertaken by General Ne Win had given rise to the wildest rumors. It was said that he had turned his country onto the Communist path, that he was on more and more intimate terms with Peking, that he was devoured by passionate anti-Westernism, almost xenophobic in its intensity.

The month hardly passed without another strange rumor being floated on the international diplomatic market. I had written General Ne Win, expressing hope that Charlotte and I might come to pay our respects. No answer. Weeks passed. Finally, a frantic cablegram reached us in Phnompenh. The Burmese representative in New York wanted to know where we could pick up our visas. We would, it was said, be able to meet with those officials whom we desired to see.

We got the visas in Bangkok but not without a sharp reminder of Burma's isolation. The Burmese consul grudgingly conceded he had authority to give me a visa but not Charlotte. When I insisted that General Ne Win had authorized visas for both of us he sneered. His cable contained no such information, he said. Finally, he condescended to ask Rangoon for instructions. The next day he rang up our hotel at half-hour intervals all day long, urgently trying to reach me. Finally, I called him back at 9:30 P.M. He was close to nervous collapse. The cable had come back from Rangoon. Obviously it was a sharp one. Indeed, he could issue a visa for Charlotte. How quickly could I pick it up?

The consul's reaction was matched by that of the Rangoon diplomatic corps. They could not believe their eyes when an American couple, a correspondent and his wife, arrived in Burma for an indefinite stay. It was big news, diplomatic news.

I do not know why General Ne Win decided to invite us to Burma. My guess is that it was connected with his own trip to the United States. It is possible to criticize Ne Win on many counts. He is subjected to strong criticism in his own country. But no one has ever said that he is not a man of utter fairness—according to his own lights. Indeed, as I came to know him and to examine Burma and the effects of his policies, it seemed more and more that his chief defects were his virtues—his complete insistence upon utter equality in all dealings, his application of every policy across the board, regardless of consequences.

This requires some explanation.

General Ne Win took power in Burma because—or so it seemed to him and his military associates—Burma was in grave peril. There were, in his opinion, two sources of the peril: corruption and inefficiency at home and danger from the Communists and the Chinese.

The Chinese threat, as he saw it, arose in a rather curious fashion. Burma had a minority of one million Chinese in a population of thirty million. The Chinese, as in most Southeast Asian countries, were concentrated in the larger cities, taking part in retail commerce, banking, trade and moneylending.

Burma had a long northern frontier with China, and this also worried Ne Win. The Burmese had poor control of the frontier area—it was the region of the Shans and the Chins, the hill tribes which had never submitted to Burmese control (a legacy, in part, of British rule, which had preferred to deal directly with the tribes and encourage their hostility toward the Burmans). The Burmese knew that the Chinese had intimate contacts with these tribes—how intimate one could never be certain. On occasion the Chinese even crossed into Burma. To be sure, the Chinese had agreed to the demarcation of most of the frontier in 1960. But this had not really brought quiet to the area.

Nor was this all. Burma had a larger and more militant and active Communist movement than any other Southeast Asian country. There were four different Communist parties in Burma, but the most active was that of the so-called "white flag" Communists. They took their ideological and tactical line from Peking. The "white flag" Communists made common cause with many of the tribal rebels. They had put armed units into the field against the Rangoon Government. These were the Communists whom Ne Win and his military associates had been fighting since 1948. They knew how strong and wily was this foe, and they were aware of the close ties between the Communists, the tribes and the Chinese.

This was enough to make a prudent ruler nervous. But it was not all. Burma had maintained friendly relations with Peking since the Chinese Communist regime was established in 1949. Burma traded with China, and because of the volume of this trade the Communist Bank of China established an office in Rangoon.

It was the activities of the Bank of China which aroused the deepest Burmese suspicions. It launched a program of loans to Chinese businessmen resident in Burma, most of them going to Chinese moneylenders in Burmese villages and to Chinese pawn-shops. The pawnshop is one of the most revered of Burmese insti-tutions. The Burman is a creature of impulse. If he wants to go to a movie and finds he hasn't the price in his pocket, he thinks nothing of taking his umbrella (a prized possession in shower-drenched Rangoon) to the pawnship. Or he will pawn his shirt or fountain pen. The pawnbroker in the Burman village wields enormous power. Together with the village moneylender, he controls the economic life of the countryside.

The tendency of the Communist bank to lend funds so that Chinese pawnbrokers and loan sharks could extend their operations into the Burman villages and the rapid acquisition by the Chinese of a stranglehold on both commerce and farmland did not go un-noticed.

Suspicions were exacerbated when China proposed to launch a major aid program. General Ne Win took a dim view of any foreign aid. He took a dimmer view of the Chinese program when he discovered that most of the Chinese funds would go to improve communications and transportation down the central route from China—the old Burma Road and the Irrawaddy waterway. As a military man it was apparent to him that once a fine highway and waterway linked Rangoon with Kunming Burma would be at the mercy of a Chinese force moving south.

Perhaps the Burmese fears were groundless. But the possibility of overt moves by a powerful neighbor controlling a strategically placed fifth column seemed no laughing matter.

What to do? Ne Win was profoundly convinced that the only safe posture for a small Asian power in the turbulence of today was neutrality. He could not act unilaterally against the Chinese. This would propel Burma to one side of the divided world. Instead, he took a step which suited him philosophically and temperamentally. The Chinese were not the only alien element in Burma. In truth, the Burmans had never conducted their own business or banking. It was in the hands of the Chinese and the Indian minority. Larger undertakings traditionally had been conducted by the British or other European countries.

Since independence Burma had followed a socialist course, and Ne Win was a supporter of what he called the Burmese path to socialism. These circumstances dictated his action. At a single stroke he nationalized all business, banking and commerce. He forbade any foreign nationals to engage in trade in Burma. Thus he cut the power of the Chinese to threaten or to conspire against his country. He also plunged Burma into an economic tailspin from which she showed no sign of emerging.

"None of us had ever had a day's economic experience," he now said wryly. By "us" he meant his fellow officers to whom he turned over the task of running the country's economy—the infantry commander suddenly put in charge of retail trade, the air force men charged with operating the newspapers, the general named to run the central bank. Socialism and government ownership were to be the order of the day—right down to the beauty parlor and the grocery store. The Chinese were forced out of business. So were the Indians. The Indians had left Burma by the hundred thousands. The Chinese had stayed. They worked for the government. Or they did nothing. Were they waiting for a turn? Possibly.

Meantime, Ne Win and his honest, blundering, naïve officers tried their best to run the economy.

"It's a mess," Ne Win said after two years of deepening economic chaos. "We have a tiger by the tail."

One foreign observer remarked bitterly: "If Ne Win is running a socialist government, it is socialism without socialists."

A walk through Rangoon's desolate streets confirmed the accuracy of Ne Win's characterization. Things were "a mess." Street after street was lined with shops whose doors and windows offered a blind and boarded-up façade. The sidewalk was broken and littered with refuse. At nightfall the commercial area became a ghost town, lighted only by scattered lamps. No restaurants, no nightclubs, no bars. For not only is Ne Win a "socialist"; he is also a puritan. Although the race track had been his dearest love, he closed that along with all other public forms of entertainment—except for the movies. The big movie houses in the heart of Rangoon became the busiest spots in town. The queues formed at eight in the morning. Why not? There was nothing else to do. The great open-air bazaar at Bakyoke had been closed—not only because of lack of goods but because it was visible evidence of the sorry state to which Burmese trade had fallen. Even if the shops had not been closed by nationalization, there was little reason to stay open—there was nothing to sell. Not even longyis, the Burmese wraparound garments, were to be had. Like almost every necessity in Burma, they were rationed—one per year to a man or woman.

It did not have to be that bad. But Ne Win was an egalitarian. He never had believed in foreign aid. Now he was more certain than ever that it was an element in foreign schemes to subvert Burmese independence.

"Unless we Burmans learn to run our own country," he told me, "we will lose it. Of course, there are hardships. But we must put our house in order."

He had a horror of what he saw happening in neighboring Southeast Asian countries where torrents of money poured in under the vast U.S. military and economic assistance programs.

"This kind of aid," he said, "does not help. It cripples. It paralyzes. The recipients never learn to do for themselves. They rely more and more on foreign experts and foreign money. In the end they lose control of their own country."

Only the strongest moral fiber, the General believed, could enable Burma to resolve her great problems. His greatest sadness was at the vanishing of the spirit of national unity and self-sacrifice which marked the struggle for Burmese independence.

He shook his head sadly. "The problems of peace are so much more difficult than those of war," he said. "Then we stood together. Now everyone is apart."

Worst of all was the problem of Burman youth. The Rangoon youngsters made every effort to follow the lead of their counterparts in London. The mods and the rockers were their ideal, though it was not easy to get Western sport shirts, skin-tight trousers and pointed Italian shoes.

They were known to the exhortatory press, somewhat to their embarrassment, as "road devils"—an old Burman term for juvenile delinquents. The press, at General Ne Win's inspiration, constantly lectured the youngsters. The authorities held condemnatory mass meetings in the schools. The films which absorbed many idle hours were strictly censored. Sophia Loren and Gina Lollobrigida were banned. But the youngsters seemed to be able to pick up the kind of ideas they wanted from such double bills as Tony Curtis in *Forty Pounds of Trouble* and Belinda Lee in *The Wild and the Wanton*.

It did not seem to me that the General was going to have much more success in holding back the tide of juvenile fad and fancy than in attempting to implant exact and precise egalitarianism in Burmese society. The day did not pass without the press reporting some such item as the action of a local distribution committee dividing up the contents of fifty-nine cans of sardines equally among a community by passing out three sardines per person. Another committee fulfilled its duty by breaking prawns into pieces and distributing them bit by bit to persons holding ration cards.

"They are trying to run Burma's economy," a diplomat said, "like a quartermaster corps in the army. One item to each soldier, regardless of need or fit."

Obviously it would not work.

Burma was one of Asia's richest agricultural countries. For many years she was Asia's largest exporter of rice. Now she had dropped to second place behind Thailand. The Thais had boosted their output, and that in Burma had fallen badly. Her exports in 1966 dropped to 1.2 million tons. Almost every necessity was rationed—rice, fish, salt, cooking oil, canned milk, soap and even prawns, the most prized delicacy in Burma. Longyis, women's skirts and umbrellas were also rationed. A family of six was allowed one man's shirt, one woman's blouse, one vest and one umbrella every six months.

The fall in rice exports had savagely curtailed Burma's foreign exchange. She depended on rice for 70 percent of her foreign exchange. This had not affected Burma's international credit. Ne Win was as prudent as Calvin Coolidge. He paid every cent of Burmese debt promptly. International bankers called Burma the Finland of the East. But the price was steep: a lack of funds to buy the machinery which Burma needed. If Burma was to hold her own in the rice trade, she needed new milling equipment. She needed new machinery for her teak harvest. Where would it come from without the foreign exchange to pay?

There could be a substantial inflow of funds through tourism. All of Burma's neighbors benefited from the golden flow of American tourist dollars. But not Burma. Tourists were not admitted. And they would flee quickly if they came. There were only two hotels, the dying Strand in the desolate commercial area and the recently built Inya Lake Hotel, erected by the Russians. The Russians put up a sign on the hotel: "Gift of the Soviet Union." When Ne Win heard of it, he insisted on paying the Russians the full cost of the hotel in rice. No charity for him.

It would not cost Ne Win much to open three or four new hotels. It would not cost much to open a bazaar and a market in downtown Rangoon and to sponsor some shops for tourist browsing. It would be easy to revive some of the closed nightclubs and bars and provide buses to take tourists about.

With a minimum investment Burma could begin to earn foreign exchange.

Charlotte suggested this to Ne Win as we sat in the great baronial dining room of his palace—the palace from which the British governor general had ruled. We were the only guests at the great mahogany table. Around us were three or four military flunkeys acting as servants. Ne Win had a security phobia. Outside on the lawn there were strands of barbed wire and great floodlights. Inside the palace there were guards with Tommy guns and clanking revolvers. We did not see any police dogs, but one of Ne Win's fellow Asian statesmen insisted he turned twenty-five savage dogs loose around the palace every night—and then made a habit of changing his sleeping place almost every evening.

There was none of that atmosphere about the dining room as we chatted cozily about Minneapolis. Minneapolis, where I grew up, was the American city Ne Win and his wife, Katie, knew best because twice he had gone there for medical treatment in the great University of Minnesota clinic.

Ne Win politely rejected Charlotte's idea that tourism offered a way out of his economic squeeze. That, he said, would mean they would have to let back in the people they had just gotten rid of— the Indian businessmen and the Chinese. It did not seem to occur to him, with his rigidly egalitarian mind, that he might let in dollar-laden Americans and keep out those foreigners whom he considered so dangerous.

He offered us a magnificent tray of fruit—mangoes, mangosteens, love apples, papayas and pineapples.

"We are considering a scheme to export our fruits to Europe," he said with a gleam. "It would require an investment of $25 or $30 million in planes and refrigeration. And we won't go into it unless we can guarantee the return of our capital in five years."

I could see this scheme appealed to him. But it seemed to epitomize the flaw in his economic thinking. I could have suggested half a dozen simple—and safer—ways of improving Burma's foreign exchange position without indulging in anything as risky and glamorous as the air fruit export business.

It seemed possible that Ne Win had begun to learn a bit about economy through the hard school of experience. There was talk of permitting a resumption of private trade in seventeen key retail categories, even if this did mean allowing some Chinese and Indians to go back into business. And the sad Armenian who had owned the Strand Hotel before its expropriation and who still ran it in lonely grandeur, dining each evening on snowy linen, gleaming silver, himself in white dinner jacket and his waiters in evening coats, had been commissioned to survey several possible sites for tourist hotels.

Whether Ne Win would permit other relaxations was not so certain. He was still keeping his political opponents under arrest, headed by the former Premier, U Nu, once his friend and associate. They were, it was said, treated well, but kept in close confinement. And there were rumors that the police had exhibited brutality toward the more independent-minded editors who had once made Burma's press the liveliest in Asia.

There was a story that Ne Win had visited U Nu and asked him what he would do if released. To which U Nu promptly replied that his initial act would be to demand Ne Win's imprisonment on charges of treason. U Nu remained under arrest, but there were signs that Ne Win felt uncomfortable about it.

Whether it was personal discomfort or complex political considerations General Ne Win was not long in giving confirmation to the rumors that U Nu would be given his liberty. Less than two months after Ne Win returned to Rangoon from his visit to the

United States in late summer U Nu was granted release from custody along with U Ba Swe, another imprisoned political leader. The general, U Nu revealed, simply appeared without notice and said, "You are free to go." "Where?" asked U Nu. "To your hearth and home," said the general.

It was conceded that by Asian standards Burma was a model of stability. Outside of Rangoon the country did not seem to be suffering from the stern economic measures. In the countryside the peasants produced their own food and most of their clothing. Rationing and shortages did not affect them as they did the urban residents. Nor was there political instability except among the restless tribes and their allies, the militant Communists.

About half of Ne Win's small army of 100,000 was in the field fighting tribal and Communist rebels. The front pages of the Rangoon papers never appeared without some item concerning the latest battles with these dissident forces.

Foreign military specialists gave Ne Win's army good marks. His officers were for the most part trained in British and American command schools. Some had gone in recent years to the Soviet Union. They were first-class men.

But, of course, Burma had no real capability for countering a major Chinese military threat. Was this a possibility? There was a sharp division of opinion. Ne Win and his associates felt that they had reduced the threat by prompt and rigorous steps. They pointed out that no country in Asia had more stable relations with all the great powers—Russia, China, the United States, Britain, India. Relations with India, which had been cool in the last days of Premier Nehru (a great friend of U Nu), warmed up under Shastri. Madame Gandhi was a close personal friend of both General and Madame Ne Win.

How well would all this serve Burma in event of a direct military threat by China? The Indians, I knew, worried considerably on this score. They sometimes thought of Burma as the great danger in their rear. The worry could be justified if the Chinese insisted on moving. But I felt that within the limits of his concepts no man could have done better at putting his country in a position to start working its way toward true independence and genuine security from subversive threat.

Ne Win was a harsh man in some ways. He told me how he once told some troops he wanted an orchid growing high in a tree. The men cut down the tree and presented him with the plant. "I wanted the orchid, but I did not want to take the life of the tree," he said. He beat the men for their conduct. He was a young officer during World War II and he had to establish his authority in difficult conditions. "I beat the men," he said. "It was necessary."

I had no doubt that he would beat his country again if he thought it was necessary for its good. But I thought also that he would fight to the last drop of his blood to keep Burma Burman and to repel any enemy no matter who or how powerful. He was a man of many faults, but lack of bravery, patriotism and dedication to his cause was not in him.

7

Bye, Bye "Hindi Chini Bhai Bhai"

THE INDIAN AIRWAYS PLANE WHICH CARRIED US FROM RANGOON TO Calcutta, was, as Charlotte observed, more like a flying nursery than a regular transport aircraft. It was crammed with refugees— Indian families, compelled to pull up stakes in Burma and return with their many children to the India of their fathers and grand- fathers. They were part of the vast human tide set in motion by General Ne Win's egalitarian drive to rid his country of all foreign tradesmen, bankers or participants in any kind of commerce. More than 300,000 Indians had already left Burma.

The refugee stream was a measure of the distance which now separated India and Burma, once the closest collaborating nations on the Asian continent.

No longer, as we were quick to discover in New Delhi, were India's ties with her Asian neighbors close and binding. To the contrary, as our driver in the Indian capital pointed out. He was a handsome, self-taught, charming young man who had grown up in a village near New Delhi and had come to the city to make his for- tune. Or at least a decent living. His parents were illiterate, but he read, wrote and spoke English well and knew his country's history. He was interested in politics, foreign affairs, diplomacy and eco- nomics. A tourist agency had offered him a job, but he hoped to go into business for himself. He was not certain exactly what business.

One day he began to talk about foreign affairs.

"Did you ever hear of 'Hindi Chini Bhai Bhai'?" he asked. "That means Indians and Chinese are brothers. That was a long time ago."

It was indeed. The Nehru slogan had been dead only four years by the calendar, but a generation in attitude. Hardly a whisper of the understanding, sympathy and compassion which marked India's attitude toward China during the first decade of the Communist regime had survived the 1962 attack and the armed confrontation which followed. Not even Krishna Menon, whose fiery partisanship for Peking so infuriated Americans, any longer had a kind word for China. Indeed, public memory of his pro-China position had virtually retired him from Indian politics.

Few Chinese remained in India and those few were compelled to masquerade as Japanese. Public hostility no longer was as hysterical as in 1962, when only signs proclaiming "I am a Japanese" protected Chinese from lynching in the Delhi streets. But the two surviving Chinese restaurants sported Japanese names—the Ginza and the Tokyo. The first page of their menus featured sukiyaki and tempura. The reverse side listed Peking duck, bird's-nest soup, ancient eggs and bamboo sprouts.

The war with China profoundly affected Indian psychology. Before I went to Delhi this had been pointed out to me both in Cambodia and in Burma. To these countries India had shone as the beacon of Asian neutralism. The spirit of Gandhi and Nehru, the doctrine of nonviolence, the whole ethic contributed to nationalist politics by the Indian independence movement was a force of enormous emotional power. It was this mixture of passion, pragmatism and philosophy on which many Asians relied to counter China's Marxism, China's violent revolutionism.

But this was now gone. In Phnompenh the pensive associates of Prince Sihanouk sadly told me that India had abandoned her neutral role and was committed to the West. This had struck them deeply. It left a sense of loss, of isolation in a deep and dangerous wilderness. Much the same feeling was expressed in Rangoon. Burma, particularly under U Nu, had practiced a mirror image of Indian neutrality. The bonds between Nehru and U Nu were warm and intimate. The two men not only shared an outlook of the world; they possessed the same religiophilosophical view. Now this unity was gone. Nehru and U Nu had passed from the scene. Their successors were good friends, but Madame Gandhi and General Ne Win did not have a common view of the world.

It was not that India had become, to use Peking's propaganda phrase, a "lackey of the Moscow-Washington conspiracy." Madame Gandhi voiced the same neutrality clichés as her father. The Indian politicians talked as though nothing had changed.

But the truth was, India had changed. It had been changed, I was convinced, by the inexorable pressure of events. Once China attacked across the Himalayan frontier, India became a different country. For the Chinese challenge threatened India's national sovereignty. She had to protect herself by any means available and she had to build her defenses, regardless of cost in philosophy or principle or material progress.

This meant turning to Russia and the U.S.A., each of which had a stake in the independence of India and her survival against China.

From that moment India lost her holy eminence of neutrality. She could not recover it. She was now an engaged power—the only state with a permanent, manned, active fighting line against the Chinese.

The more sophisticated Indian leaders, associates of Madame Gandhi, were quick to explain to me that Indian neutrality was one of the major targets of the Chinese attack.

The Chinese assault, they felt, had been conceived with devilish cunning and had a variety of objectives. It was designed to drive India from her neutral position and compel her to fall into tacit or open alliance with the West. The Chinese hoped to exploit this forced shift by supplanting India as adviser, mentor and model for the uncommitted nations of Asia and Africa.

A deeper Chinese purpose, some of Madame Gandhi's associates felt, was to shove India's precarious economy off balance, by compelling her to spend much more on arms and reduce her investment in capital industries. The Chinese, confronted by economic hazards of their own, hoped to prevent India from emerging as the economic model which other backward countries might emulate. By intensifying India's economic problems the Chinese could slow her down, and thus reap an advantage for themselves. They also sought to sow dissent, political unrest and economic hardship. This would weaken India as a political rival in Asia.

Only peripherally, these Indians believed, did the Chinese desire to recover the barren and icecapped wastelands of the Himalayas which they claimed as theirs.

The conquest of the land, however, possessed a significance of major import. These frontiers had been in dispute for many years. The Chinese claims were genuine and incidentally had the support of Chinese Nationalists (as they had themselves told me) as well as Communists. By taking the territory from India the Chinese were demonstrating to their own people their ability to achieve China's nationalistic territorial aspirations. Not yet, perhaps, were they strong enough to do this all around the periphery. But they were strong enough to do it in a distant corner of Asia. This, of course, was a lesson not to be lost on other Asian nations. It might be expected to enhance China's power image while injuring that of India.

By making good their claim to the Himalayan hinterland the Chinese gave credibility to their other territorial claims. They might still be a long way from repossessing the vast lands which they insisted had been wrested from successive Chinese emperors by the Russians. But they put the Russians, their own peoples and those of the Asian countries on notice that they were prepared where necessary (and desirable) to back their claims with armed force.

Russia was involved in another fashion in the Chinese calculations. Peking put the Russians on the horns of a dilemma. If Moscow supported India, the Chinese could claim that the Soviet Union had assisted a non-Communist power against a member of the Communist camp. If Moscow did not support India, the Chinese were prepared to point out to the other neutralist, noncommitted nations the hazards of attempting to rely on Russia for support. Only by joining the Chinese bloc, the argument would run, are you certain of support.

India's transformation from the role of idealistic pacifist to that of engaged belligerent, locked in military confrontation with her great Asian rival, occurred so swiftly that the Indians found it difficult to adjust to the implications.

One evening I talked with two New Delhi editors. The conversation gravitated to the Vietnam war.

"It's very curious," one said, "but India is not taking the lead in bringing peace to Vietnam. I don't know what has happened to us."

I agreed. Vietnam was not mentioned as often in conversation in New Delhi as it was in Rangoon or Phnompenh or Bangkok. Nor was it reflected in the press. News coverage was lackadaisical, uninspired. There were (or so it appeared) no Indian journalists in Vietnam. It was not a subject which preoccupied the public.

"There doesn't seem to be any bite to your attitude on Vietnam," I said. "What has happened to India's great role as keeper of the world's conscience?"

"We're too preoccupied with our own affairs," one editor said.

"It's our fault as editors," said the other. "We must write more about it and stir the public up."

They decided to try to stimulate a new Indian initiative for a Vietnam truce. In the next week each published vigorous editorials. They tried to rouse their associates. They made tentative plans for a mass meeting. Nothing came of it.

Nothing came, either, of Madame Gandhi's more formal initiatives. She joined with Prime Minister Harold Wilson in one effort. She went to Moscow in July and issued a joint communiqué with the Soviet leaders just after I visited New Delhi. So far as the Indian public was concerned there was only a flicker of interest. Vietnam roared dangerously along. India was oblivious.

I felt that a tragic reason underlay India's paralysis on Vietnam. India no longer possessed the power to stir the world's moral sensibilities. Not because Gandhi had been replaced by Nehru and then by Shastri and Madame Gandhi. Not because of defects in Madame Gandhi's character or lack of charisma. But because India no longer stood on a pulpit. No longer could she look from a pinnacle of moral rectitude and command the world's attention. Now she herself was down in the arena, deeply engaged. So long as she was, perforce, a belligerent power, at war with China and dependent upon the United States and the Soviet Union for arms, aid and matériel she could not muster the moral force to move men's hearts and pierce men's minds. She could not mount the stage of the United Nations and bring down the lightning on those who resorted to war. For she herself was living by the sword.

In practical terms this meant that India must maintain a precarious balance with both the United States and the Soviet Union. If Madame Gandhi was compelled, by urgent need of economic assistance from the United States (and the need of preventing U.S. arms from flowing once again to her enemy and China's ally, Pakistan), to accept a conservative, deflationary fiscal program, providing for devaluation of the rupee (to increase exports) and relaxations on import quotas (to encourage imports), she was promptly compelled to pay a state visit to Moscow to show the Soviets that she was as much their friend as she was Washington's. If Moscow opposed the American-devised economic program, Madame Gandhi must redress the balance by backing the Soviet position on Vietnam.

Only by intricate maneuvers could India be certain of receiving the flow of loans and technical assistance needed for her economy, the military advice and experts to cope with complex problems of mountain warfare—not to mention the modern weapons of war with which to hold back the Chinese.

It was not easy.

Yet, in a sense, the military aspect was not India's most difficult problem. Far more difficult was the question of population.

Charlotte and I went to call on Colonel B. L. Raina, commander in chief of India's population control drive. We found him in a dingy office in a remodeled villa on the outskirts of Delhi. We had seen on billboards throughout Delhi a striking poster of a woman holding in her hand a small bit of coiled plastic. It bore the legend, "Use Loop For Family Planning." The sign was posted both in English and Hindi. Now as Colonel Raina, a solid balding man, rose from his desk, we saw twirling in his hand an actual loop.

Colonel Raina was a former military surgeon whose life had been devoted to population control for thirty years—ever since he attended a lecture by Margaret Sanger in 1936 and became convinced that only by massive reduction of India's birth rate would it be possible to solve her social and economic problems. Within a year he had formed his own small "Health of a Mother Society," and now with the launching of a national program of birth control Colonel Raina had been picked to carry the campaign to the people.

This he was doing with energy, resolution, enormous goodwill, considerable humor but some lack of tact and little sensitivity—factors which he probably felt had no place in the crash program he had launched.

It was his ambition to insert six million loops in the 1966–67 biennial. He believed that he would hit the one million figure by the anniversary of the start of his drive in autumn, 1966. By 1971 he hoped to begin to affect India's birth rate in a material manner. When and if he could reach the total of sixty million insertions, the Indian population would be stabilized. At present India had a birth rate of 40 per 1,000, a death rate of 17 per 1,000, an excess of 23 per 1,000. Her population reached the 500 million mark in 1966, increasing at a rate of 11 million a year. In ten years India had added to the world the equivalent of the populations of Great Britain and Germany.

As Colonel Raina talked he toyed with his loop. Around and

around his finger it spun. This was part calculated tactic, part nervousness. He conceded that he faced an infinity of difficulties—the fact that 10 percent of the loops were expelled, that another 10 percent had to be removed, that a certain percentage of women already were pregnant when the loop was installed. Nonetheless the insertions were, he said, about 78 percent effective. True, they sometimes caused bleeding (actually, rather more often than not). True, there were critics who said he was offering a "cafeteria" program. True, there were areas in India where the program was sharply resisted, had not even gotten off the ground. True, there had been criticism about some of his tactics—the gathering of women into camps for mass insertions, the harshness (brutality, some said) of doctors, the difficulty of getting village midwives to participate. Despite all this Colonel Raina was utterly confident that his program would work. He cited Taiwan and South Korea as examples of countries where similar programs already had begun to affect population growth.

But he did not minimize the difficulties, particularly the length of time required before the program began to bite into the birth rate. To prevent one birth, he conceded, loops must be inserted in five fertile women.

While he estimated that sixty million insertions would stabilize India's population, the total will probably have passed 600 million before that figure can be achieved. If the population reached a higher figure before the sixty-million rate was achieved, it simply meant that more loops would be required. It was a good deal like trying to empty a swimming pool with an eyedropper. But Colonel Raina did not seem to lose his enthusiasm.

His goal was to cut back India's birth rate to about 25 per 1,000. He knew that this would require not only loops but also sterilization, probably legalized abortion and millions of conventional birth control devices. It would require discouraging the practice of widow remarriage, a lifting of the normal marriage age (a boost to twenty-five would cut the birth rate by one-quarter), and social changes which would reduce economic incentives for producing so many children.

Yet there was no alternative, in Colonel Raina's opinion. India possessed only 2.4 percent of the world's land area, much of it utterly useless for agriculture (mountains, deserts, unfertile plains, tropical jungles), and 14 percent of the world's population. She lived in entire dependence on the Western world for foodstuffs. Were American aid to be cut off for one month, starvation would begin. In 1965 mass starvation because of the massive crop failure—it was thirteen million tons short—was avoided only by a remarkable American achievement in shipping in wheat backed by an equally remarkable Indian achievement in distributing it to the famine points.

Yet India possessed the power to feed herself. Each year she lost one-fifth of her crop to rats, to pests, to rot, to mold, to inefficient harvest methods, to faulty storage (or lack of storage), to the absence of modern means of shipment and distribution. If that grain could be saved, India need fear no famine.

The appalling figure bedeviled the experts until they began to realize that if India had the modern facilities to conserve her food she would also have the capability of doing many other things: to radically increase her harvest yields through better seed, fertilizer, methods and mechanization; to control or reduce her population, etc.

The harsh fact was that the rats and insects and molds got the food because India had not the capability of preventing such loss. And without that she could not feed herself.

American wheat shipments saved India from disaster after the crop failure of 1965. But they provided no margin of safety. India went into the summer of 1966 tense and nervous. From the middle of June onward everyone watched for the rains. If the rains did not come, if the monsoon failed, India was headed for catastrophe. And this would be a catastrophe from which no one could save her. For there was no more storage capacity for grains from America.

Nor means of sending more. Nor did America possess the reserves which would be needed in event of another disaster.

Everything hinged on the rains—not only India's economy, India's ability to supply her armies, her ability to resist China, the viability of her liberal socialist orientation, the fate of Madame Gandhi's government, the capacity of the Congress Party to hold the Communist movement in check. Beyond this at stake was India's future as a national state, and the lives of millions of her people.

Seldom had so much depended upon the rains.

Nor would the drama end with the drenching downpours of the summer of 1966. These might save the day for the moment. In 1967 the same cruel drama would begin again. There was no end to it. There would be no end to it until by some means India could bring her food and population into equilibrium.

This was perceived by most of India's planners. It was understood by Ambassador Chester Bowles and the team of Americans who sought to help India cope with the dilemma. On both sides there dawned the realization that not just India faced the tragedy of too little food. It was the world. India's plight, as Ambassador Bowles explained, was not unrelated to that of the other great countries which had demonstrated in recent years a persistent inability to produce enough to feed their peoples—notably, Russia and China. India had to stand in line along with the other huge population aggregates—three nations with a total population of 1.4 billion—the three largest nations in the world, each chronically short of food and growing shorter, each dependent upon the grain-surplus nations, the United States, Canada and Australia.

Events had taken a strange and dangerous turn. The sudden rise of demand from India and the other grain-short nations had caught the grain-surplus countries, especially the United States, off guard. For years the United States had struggled to reduce its grain production, to halt the creation of staggering additions to the already towering surpluses. Now, with crop controls still rigidly enforced, with elaborate bonuses still paid to hold down production, it became apparent that the bottom of the barrel was in sight. Not only was American capacity to aid deficit countries like India jeopardized; there was the appalling prospect that a short crop in any surplus country plus a failure in any deficit country would bring on famine comparable to those which once were "China's sorrow." No one in the world would have the food to tide the stricken land over the barren months.

Nowhere was this more vividly appreciated than in India. And in no other respect was there so great an impingement upon India's freedom of political action. If she was dependent upon Moscow and Washington for military aid to defend herself against China, she was even more dependent upon the United States for food to avert total disaster.

Small wonder that India's voice no longer sounded over the materialist world like a trumpet of moral destiny. India's life depended on materials which only other powers could provide.

One vestige of India's moral superiority remained: her demand for an end to nuclear weapons and banishment of the threat of nuclear war. She could still speak to the world across the heads of the entangled diplomats at Geneva and demand that the world forswear these fateful weapons.

Yet even here there were those who felt they could detect a waning of Indian fervor.

Time was running out on India's nuclear clock. China's bomb and China's nuclear capability had worked in deadly fashion to undermine the Indian principle of ban-the-bomb. Since 1964 the debate had been moving out of the shadows and into the public arena. Still, no reputable Indian public figure would tell me for quotation that India must possess the bomb. Still, the heritage of Gandhi and Nehru was too strong. Yet a foreigner who had watched the Indian scene for many years said quietly: "They'll get a bang of one sort or another within a few years." Another estimated that India would have the bomb within three to five years.

India had the know-how to create the bomb. The Indian public wanted the bomb—had wanted it ever since the first China bomb test, had wanted it even more after the second test, had demanded it after the third and fourth tests in 1966.

What held India back? The government and her political figures, clinging to the heritage of Gandhi, to the last shreds of Indian pacifism. But there seemed little chance that this attitude would long continue. India's Defense Minister Chavan told me frankly: "China's nuclear weapon is a direct threat to us. She needs no special capability to deliver it on India—just an ordinary bomber, taking off from Lhasa, can drop it on Delhi." He insisted that India's nuclear policy was unchanged. Of course, he added, if the negotiations in Geneva failed, if there was no nonproliferation treaty, naturally India would have to re-examine her position.

India had all the technical knowledge needed to make the bomb. She even had cost estimates—surprisingly low ones, ranging to $30 and $40 million. She possessed no source of fissionable materials herself. She produced plutonium but only through the reactor which she operated in collaboration with the Canadians under an agreement that the product was not to be used for military purposes. However, India did possess natural uranium. She would manage with that, the experts said. They did not think India would produce many nuclear weapons. But she could certainly turn out enough to become a member of the nuclear club within a very few years. Certainly, I was told, she would have no trouble in arming herself with a *force de frappe*—against China.

Once that occurred, the last vestige of Gandhi's heritage would, for practical purposes, vanish from her national policy. But not, perhaps, from the mythology of her politics.

Would this have occurred without China? Perhaps. But there was no doubt in my mind that China was a catalyst which was producing a political chain reaction in India equal in magnitude to any which the cyclotron in the University of Chicago Field House had started.

8

Essentially a Mountainous Country

THE ROAD FROM BAGHDOGRA LEADS UP. AT FIRST THE GRADE IS GENTLE and the macadam winds through tall well-tended teak forests, now sheltering camp after camp of Indian Army units—truck depots, supply companies, infantry units, hospitals, one after another, an almost continuous military establishment. Signs proclaim it a forest district, a reserve. The trees carry marks, indicating type and age. Amongst them masses of flamboyants plunge like balls of flame; overhanging limbs sag under sprays of (what looked to me like) giant Easter lilies, broken by seas of azaleas, pink and blooming.

But always the road led up.

Two men met us at the airport. Small men, not much more than five feet tall, with round heads and children's open smiles. They were compact neat bundles of muscles, more like large dwarfs than small men. They reminded me of Sherpas. But they were not. They were Sikkimese—to be correct they were Bhutia-Lepchas—and they came from the palace in Sikkim. Businesslike, they bustled about, collecting luggage, getting passports stamped, handing us the "Inner Line permits" required by the Indian Government of any traveler who wishes to proceed beyond Kalimpong or Darjeeling, up to the Himalayas.

Then we climbed into the palace jeep with its big SIK license plate and drove away from the airport and into Kalimpong. We

95

dropped one small Sikkimese man, picked up a bag of groceries for the palace, and took the road for Rangpo. It was a good road and the traffic was almost exclusively military—truck columns, jeeps. From the moment we landed at Baghdogra we felt we had entered a military base. There were, according to a good but unofficial estimate, 25,000 to 50,000 troops jammed into reserve camps and supply stations in the approach areas to Assam, Sikkim and Bhutan. Most of them were in barracks or semipermanent tent camps. It looked as though the Indian Army counted on being there a long time.

The road led up through foothills, gradually moving onto higher ground. We began to see tea terraces on the tall hills along the course where the Tista River cut through the stone mountain cliffs in a reckless torrent of amber and gray. The Tista was heavy with fine silt and foamed around the great boulders like breakers on the coast of Maine.

The road led up, still tar, still smooth, still well maintained. The Sikkimese driver pushed the jeep hard. He spoke no English and his face was a mask, concentrated on the single task of driving. His companion had said the trip would take at least five hours because floods had cut Sikkim's connections with the outer world the week before and only a roundabout secondary road had been restored.

The road led up, and finally we came to a halt at the Inner Line, where our permit was inspected. On to Rangpo, the frontier of Sikkim. Another halt. Another Inner Line permit inspection. As we waited, a siren sounded up the highway and a red-painted Indian Army jeep roared through, slowing but not halting, and rattled over the Tista River bridge. It was the command jeep of the Indian major general in charge of the Sikkim front, a tall, handsome cavalryman who later apologized for the noise and ostentation of his siren and for not giving us a lift to Gangtok.

We tagged on behind the flashy jeep, across the bridge and up a steep grade to an open square where a large sign greeted us: "Sikkim Distilleries." This was the largest industrial enterprise in the kingdom, supplying gin, whiskey, cordials, liqueurs and brandy to the Indian trade. Whatever your need, Sikkim Distilleries could fill it, and on short notice.

On up led the road. No longer macadam, except in patches. Mostly gravel, narrowing to tiny ledges cut from the granite mountainsides. Up, up, up, switchback after switchback. Up a mountainside by switchback, then down by switchback, across the stream and up the other side. Up, up, up past the cloud line and into watery fog. Higher and higher on the mountainsides mounted the terraces, rice and corn. Tall corn—seven, eight or nine feet tall, the kind that has not been seen in Iowa in a generation or more. Rice sets, green as the inside of an Irishman's heart, in geometric rows, growing at seven thousand feet. Corn marching up to nine thousand. Irrigation waters dripping row by planted row down the mountainside from the perpetual clouds of nine thousand, to eight thousand, to seven thousand feet. . . .

It grew cold and dark, and now we were driving continuously in the Himalayan cloud, the road narrower than ever, often undercut, hastily repaired, half sliding down the ax-steep cliffs after last week's floods. The fog thickened, the cold sharpened, the dark deepened.

And then lights flickered high on the mountain across a valley. We worked our way upward on the switchbacks, and now the lights sprayed out to cover the peak like a giant's Christmas tree. This was Gangtok, a sparkle of surprise set in drifting cotton wool. Barracks jutted from the highest cliff—the Indian Army encampment. Then a paved road, a row of bazaars and a dozen improbable pipers in kilts and tartans straggling up the hill toward the palace, a wraith of a villa picked out of the foggy cloud by floodlights.

It was after 8 P.M. We had driven for six hours almost straight up the wall of the Himalayas and now had come to the capital of the most remote kingdom in the world, to the palace of its king; and the Gyalmo, Hope Cooke, was whispering us welcome (and telling us of her birthday, for which the pipers were to play), and the Chogyal, her husband, handsome, warm and casual, was showing us to our rooms.

The distance from the Inner Line to Gangtok, as a hawk flies, is less than twenty-five miles. But as the switchbacks climb the Himalayas, it was five hard hours of driving.

P. N. Bose, deputy superintendent of the Geological Survey of India, describes Sikkim in these terms: "Sikkim is essentially a mountainous country without a flat piece of land of any extent anywhere."

His description is terse and accurate. Later we saw the flattest piece of land in Sikkim—the only flat piece of land—a strip in Gangtok just wide and long enough for a football field. A game was in progress, the Sikkim Guards against Darjeeling. Most of the spectators watched the game from the mountainside—no room beside the field for bleachers. There is no landing strip in Sikkim. The only way to build one would be to cut off the top of a mountain.

For centuries Sikkim led the obscure life of the Himalayas, a link in the lavaliere of mountain kingdoms that fringed India's northern littoral. To the west lay Nepal and Kashmir, to the east Bhutan and the hill principalities of the Nagas and the Mizos, to the north the inscrutable face of Tibet.

In the Himalayas each mountain fastness has more in common with the other than with lands beyond the peaks. This is the roof of the world, the land of mountains, of eternal snow, of goat-men who live and work at heights of sixteen and eighteen thousand feet, of fog and snows, of floods and fastnesses. Here tower the incredible peaks of Kanchenchunga, of Everest, of a dozen others eternally lost in clouds. Here the trails pass through eighteen-thousand-foot passes to Tibet, to Lhasa, to the forbidden lands beyond the highest mountains.

The smallest and most isolated of the roof-of-the-world kingdoms was Sikkim, almost unheard of before the fairy tale of the Chogyal and Hope Cooke put Sikkim's name on page one.

Now a circumstance far more serious, far more significant, had encompassed the tiny kingdom. Along Sikkim's high passes to Tibet Indian troops stood guard in concrete abutments, looking across a narrow no-man's land, to Chinese pillboxes and Chinese Army emplacements. This—with Ladakh—was an active Indian-Chinese front, the scene of confrontation, vigilance, skirmishes.

A half-century ago Sir Halford Mackinder, the founder of geopolitics, proclaimed a quasi-mystical doctrine, the doctrine of the Heartland. "Who rules the Heartland," he said, "rules Asia. Who rules Asia rules the world."

This was the very heart of Heartland—this grim and forbidding massif, this eruption of the world's greatest mountains—the Pamirs, the Himalayas, the Tien Shan. This was the inner circle, the mountainous mecca toward which the visionaries of the world and so many of its conquerors had been irresistibly attracted.

Whatever the validity of Mackinder's doctrine, the roof of the world had been the center of a swaying and complex power struggle since the late nineteenth century. First Britain, then Russia contended for it. Then they agreed to a division and a balance. The Russians firmly held the old silk caravan routes to the north and the passes leading south—the emirates of Bokhara, Samarkand, the great oasis of Tashkent, the approaches to the black sands of Kashgar. Russia took under her protection Mongolia, the Gobi and the lost shrine of Karakorum. Afghanistan was made neutral ground. So was Tibet. But England won for India the trade routes to Lhasa, the routes that led through Sikkim.

So the balance held. It survived World War I and even World War II. Communists displaced the czars, England yielded place to India, but the division of the Heartland continued.

In none of these arrangements was China consulted. There was no Chinese zone of influence, no Chinese role.

Yet before the rise of Imperial Russia and Imperial Britain, China ruled the Heartland. The fastness of Tibet paid tribute to Peking. The mountain kingdoms of the Himalayas sent *corvées* of gold and slaves. So did the emirates of Central Asia, the nomads of the black sands. The Mongols first kowtowed to the Celestial power, then seized and wielded it themselves.

The realization of change, the Chogyal told me, came slowly to the Himalayas. The rise of Communism in China was hardly noted in Gangtok, Katmandu, Bhutan, Lhasa. To the handkerchief kingdom of Sikkim—forty miles wide, one hundred miles long—India's independence was far more significant than establishment of Communist power in Peking. Sikkim had been a British protectorate. Now the elderly Chogyal, father of the present prince, agreed to a new treaty, placing Sikkimese foreign relations, defense and supervisory control of internal affairs in Indian hands. The status of each Himalayan kingdom differed. Bhutan let India manage foreign affairs but kept defense in its own hands. Nepal possessed full independence and managed its own foreign affairs and army. Kashmir was a disputed area between India and Pakistan. Tibet waited in metaphysical tranquillity beyond the mountain barrier.

If Sikkim had a reason for existence, it was Tibet. The trails to Lhasa led out of the Sikkim mountains, up the Chumbi Valley, which once, in long-lost history, had been Sikkimese, and on to Lhasa. Sikkim's rulers were intimately connected with Tibet. The Chogyal's mother was Tibetan. His wife was Tibetan. The ruling house was interlocked by marriage and linked by mutual interest with the great families of Tibet, monastic and princely.

The Sikkimese house was related, too, to that of Bhutan. And there were close connections with Nepal, which accounted for 75 percent of Sikkim's 160,000 population, the rest being Bhutanese, Tibetan or what were called Bhutia-Lepcha.

The great changes in Peking first were dimly echoed in Tibet, then more strongly. Alarm spread. The Dalai Lama fled. But India counseled patience, conciliation. It was the high noon of "Hindi Chini Bhai Bhai." The Dalai Lama returned to Lhasa and cautious coexistence was attempted. All this time, said the Chogyal, Sikkim watched nervously. But the caravans still moved north. The herds ranged back and forth across the distant seventeen-thousand-foot frontier between Sikkim and Tibet where three Sikkim policemen sufficed to maintain order. In Sikkim itself there was a company of Indian troops, 160 men, and the Sikkim Guards, 300 strong. The Chogyal twice made remarkable expeditions to Tibet, once in 1954 with his Tibetan wife, again in 1956, the first trip by horseback caravan, the second by jeep. He and his party camped on the open steppe, crossed the high passes, lived in the lamaseries (the Chogyal, himself, was a second-degree incarnation, and ruled not only as an autocrat but as a theocrat), attended the sacred rites of the high temples, photographing it all in color, even the macabre antics of the Supreme Oracle, struggling in frenzy to hurl himself on the flaming pyre of objects he had cast into the fire amid mad incantations.

Sikkim's role as purveyor to Tibet continued almost unchanged. The caravans came up from Kalimpong and on through Kupup to New Yatung. Others outfitted at Gangtok for the journey through the high passes, then set out for Nathu la, the Chumbi Valley and Gyantse. From this trade issued more than 70 percent of Sikkim's revenues. The Chogyal had a stake in it. The state set up a company which held a monopoly of highway transport to Tibet. Sikkim sold to Tibet grain and rice and consumer goods from India. In return she got salt and tea.

But menace crept over the high peaks. Uneasy coexistence in Tibet grew more uneasy. When the Dalai Lama fled and civil war broke out in 1959, contacts across the frontier grew difficult. Five thousand Tibetans fled into Sikkim and won a precarious shelter. Gradually the Indians built up the strength of their Sikkim force, from the 130-man company of 1949 to a battalion, and then by 1956 to a brigade. But still the north remained open and free of access. Trade continued. There were twelve Sikkimese police, each with a rifle and fifty cartridges, on the border in the open summer, three in the icy nightmare of winter. Why should there be more? No one, the Chogyal said, could move across the high mountain trails. And if they did, there was no means of going farther, no communications, no food, no shelter, no roads.

Then came 1962—the Chinese attack on India. The attack was to the west—in the north face of Kashmir at Ladakh and across the high Himalayan passes. But the alarm rang along the whole mountain glacis. Indian troops poured into Sikkim until there were 25,000 to 30,000 now, guarding the passes to Tibet. No more trade for Sikkim, the border sealed tight. An end to the pastoral movement of sheep and goats across the passes in the north—and with it loss of livelihood, an end to a way of life.

And harsh economic and political repercussions for Sikkim. The Tibet forwarding trade was gone. So was the trade in animals, wool, hides and meat. Sikkim had never been self-sufficient in food, scraping a narrow existence out of the terraced corn and rice, long barred from tea by British determination to keep a monopoly for Darjeeling and Assam.

There was one balancing circumstance. The Indian troops brought business. The building of a net of roads and trails to supply the mountain positions brought work.

But the Indians were a mixed blessing. They did not bother to conceal their wish that Sikkim be incorporated into India. They looked with suspicion and hostility on the Chogyal's determination to maintain Sikkim's independence and to increase, if possible, her area of sovereignty. Sikkim, they said, was too small, too poor, too backward to handle its own affairs. It was, it was hinted, a possible security risk as well. After all, there were the well-known links of the Sikkim ruling house to Tibet and the Chogyal's intimate association with the Tibet trade.

The fairy tale of the Chogyal and his American bride made headlines in the United States. It aroused little pleasure in New Delhi, especially when it became evident that the American interest in Sikkim captured by the spectacle of a Sarah Lawrence girl sharing the throne of a remote Himalayan kingdom was not likely soon to die. More worrisome to calculating Foreign Office underlings was the prospect that a move by India to incorporate Sikkim into India would now evoke a sharp and angry American reaction.

The politics of the Himalayas, I found by listening to the Chogyal as he drove around his kingdom, his strong hands skillfully maneuvering the jeep over precarious ledges, across roaring torrents which turned sheer seven-thousand-foot cliffs into dangerous fords, bore considerable resemblance to the politics of the prewar Balkans or the old Irish wards of Boston. It was a difficult, chancy business, dangerous at times, always delicate. A web of relationships connected the mountain kingdoms. When the Premier of Bhutan was murdered, it shook Sikkim and Nepal. For the Premier's wife was the Chogyal's aunt. And the accused assassins found refuge in Katmandu. Nor did the game halt at the China frontier. Radio Lhasa made veiled references to the "illegitimate" ruler of Sikkim. The words were perfectly understood in the Himalayas. For there existed a senior line of Sikkim's royal Namgyel house, and the present Chogyal was descended from a junior line. It was well known in Katmandu, in Gangtok, in Bhutan and in Lhasa that two princes of the senior line still lived in Tibet.

When India sealed the border with Tibet in 1962, expelling China's consuls, and when China deported the last Indian trading agent from Tibet and closed India's consulates, the Tibetan trade did not halt, although for some months Tibet suffered very seriously. New routes from Nepal were opened, longer but perfectly adequate. For Nepal maintained a careful neutrality with China—to India's concern and resentment. And now a fine highway connected Katmandu with the Tibet frontier, built with Chinese assistance, to facilitate trade. And, as the Indians wryly warned, to serve as an invasion route when and if China decided to strike.

China already had moved twice on the Himalayan frontier—first in 1962 in Kashmir, then in the autumn of 1965 in Sikkim. Would she strike again? This was possible. Indian troops stared across the barbed wire and bunkers at Chinese troops. The posts on either side ran up to eighteen-thousand-foot elevations, so high the troops, although they could survive, could hardly fight or carry on other activities.

But the Indian forces were a far cry from those which straggled back under the blows of the Chinese attack in 1962. Today, an American specialist told me, they were the finest, toughest, hardiest, best-equipped mountain troops in the world, backed by a network of five thousand miles of lateral interconnecting mountain roads, permitting rapid supply, reinforcement and transfer.

They were capable, in his opinion, of containing any attack the Chinese might mount, short of an assault launched by stupendously reinforced armies. The Indians could muster more than 300,000 men against the Chinese in the Ladakh area. They had 25,000 on the lines in Sikkim, and the backup force in Assam and Darjeeling could quickly double or triple the Sikkim force.

The Chinese in Tibet had by the summer of 1966 reduced their troop dispositions considerably. Defense Minister Chavan gave me an estimate of 125,000 to 140,000. The Chogyal thought the figure was twelve divisions—possibly 150,000. An independent estimate put it closer to twelve regiments than twelve divisions.

Whatever the precise numbers, the truth was that I found the Himalayan fronts in 1966 quiet and dull. True, the Chinese steadily worked to increase their air capability, particularly in the Lhasa region. True, they continued to increase their road networks. But they had pulled troops out of the Sikkim front and they had remained static at Ladakh.

Fear of new action on the high Himalayas had not vanished. There was Nepal, for instance—open, exposed, with a pleasant valley and a fine highway leading to Katmandu. There was Bhutan, still maintaining its own defense—or a fiction of it. It had possibly twelve thousand troops, but the soldiers really were rather less than militia and not all had guns. There was a tiny Indian Army training mission there, but no real capability if China attacked. There were two resources: the Indian Army reserves which I saw in Assam and Darjeeling and the Bhutanese frontier with Tibet—so precipitous, so high, so dangerous that it was pierced by no normal trade route or trails for nomadic herders. There was concern, too, about the defense of Assam should China strike there. For here India had a serious border problem—unrest, deep grievances, revolt and rebellion among the Naga and Mizo tribesmen. Someday the Chinese might make common cause with the hill people. And when they did the Himalayan defenses could be flanked.

When I talked to the peoples of the Himalayas I found that Mackinder's doctrine of the Heartland encompassed a concept totally alien to their thought. As far back as history went, there had been fighting for the passes. As far back as memory recorded, tribes and kingdoms had waxed and waned. Two great powers had always contended for the roof of the world—China and India—but usually at such a far remove that it was the relationships of the clans or nomadic groupings across the nearest mountain range which bore more weight.

The greatest presence was not military and its center was not China, not India. The presence was that of the yellow sect of the Buddhist faith, the great doctrine which had its spiritual home in the most remote and forbidden capital of the world—Lhasa. It was yellow Buddhism, the faith, the philosophy, the priesthood, the superstition and the belief which gave a common denominator to the roof of the world. One day we went with the Chogyal and the Gyalmo to Rangacholing monastery. We rode in jeeps and then on horseback up the stony and slippery trail to the very peak of Rangacholing Mountain, to a forest of prayer flags fluttering white as ghosts in the fog. The stone stupas rose strong and gray against the sky. Four years ago the monastery, one of the most ancient in Sikkim, had burned. Now the Chogyal was dedicating a new structure. The priests chanted their long prayers, their robes flashing maroon and saffron, the heavy drums beating, the long horns sounding and the chant of the monks repetitive and onomatopoetic. There was a smell of incense and fresh-cut juniper. At each corner the Chogyal and the Gyalmo put down a stone. They put one down in the center and then another between each two already laid. The prayer flags flew—yellow at the east, white at the south, red at the west and blue at the north, the symbols of earth, of air, of fire, of water.

The ceremony was in Sikkim. But the scene might have been

two thousand miles to the north in the legend-haunted ruins of Karakorum, or a thousand miles to the east in the deserts of Sinkiang, or a thousand miles to the west in the fastness of the Pamirs.

For this was the Buddhist bond universal which gave to the roof of the world a unity and a significance which transcended the empires of the West and the new empires of the East. Today and for the foreseeable future Lhasa, the capital of the Inner Kingdom, was immobile, occupied, oppressed, its temples devastated, its priests persecuted, its faith challenged. But peering out into the white fog which cloaked the unearthly profile of Kanchenchunga, I could not but wonder. Did not the Heartland possess a continuity which would transcend the ephemeral ebb and flow of alien forces? Might not the Heartland possess other secrets than that postulated by Mackinder?

We saw the Himalayas as a fighting front, real and potential, between the Indians on the one side and the Chinese on the other. We saw it as a scene of the struggle for power between the Russians, the Chinese, the Americans, the Indians. This was its context in the later part of the twentieth century. But one could not live long in a land which reached so close to heaven without beginning to think in more than temporal terms. There were, it seemed to me, secrets of humanity locked in these high temples which man would still be struggling to unlock ten thousand years from now, long after the ashes of history had buried the issues and principles which so conflicted our thinking today, long after the very names of our empires and the philosophies for which they stood had eroded from the consciousness of humanity. Here on the earth's roof one knew that time was an eternity and life but a fleeting second.

9

A Statue of Stalin

THE OLD PILGRIMAGE ROUTE TO MONGOLIA RUNS NORTH FROM SIKKIM, up the high passes to the Tibetan plateau, on to Lhasa and then over a thousand miles of mountain and desert across the Gobi and into the uplands of the Orkhon and the Selenga. With good camels and ponies the journey from Gangtok to Ulan Bator was often made in four or five months.

It's another story today. To get from Gangtok to Ulan Bator Charlotte and I had, first, to pick our way down from the Himalayan heights over thunderous mountain slides which blocked the road at half a dozen points. With a relay of Indian Army jeeps which waited on either side of the caved-in mountain ledges we managed to descend from Sikkim to the steaming plain at Baghdogra. But this was just a starter. Then came a plane flight to Calcutta. Another to New Delhi. A daylong flight straight over the deserts of Pakistan, the peaks of Afghanistan, the high Pamirs and on across the steppe to Moscow. A long night's air journey eastward to Irkutsk and a final short hop south to Ulan Bator—thirty-six hours of elapsed travel time and a journey six times longer than the ancient caravan path.

It was a harassed and hurried trip. Harassed by visa difficulties and hurried in order to reach Mongolia for the national holidays.

Since the days of Genghis Khan the great holiday of the Mongols

107

has been held in early summer—in the July days when the upland meadows of the high plateaus are knee-deep in new grass, when the flocks of sheep have been moved up from the wintering lowlands and the herds of horses have begun to sleek out in the rich pastures and the warm sun. I was determined that Charlotte should see Mongolia in this halcyon period.

Mongolia is a land of harsh contrast—of 50-and-60-degree-below-zero temperatures in winter, of baking heat in summer. The worst season is the spring, when the thin snow cover has vanished and fierce winds scourge the steppe, driving the flinty dust in clouds that obscure the sun, envelop the canvas-covered yurts and penetrate the lungs. The toll is heavy, especially among the young, who fall easy prey to pneumonia as they crawl about the yurts in the chill winds, the dustladen air.

But by June the weather has changed. The sun has warmed the high plateaus. The meadows lose their winter brown, and the annual trek of the Mongols, their animals and their portable felt conical tents begins, the traditional move from lowland to highland.

In July comes a pause. This is the time when Mongolia's rains fall, gentle showers that alternate with sunshine a half-dozen times a day. Now the herds are established on the good pastures and there is time for relaxation, for rest, for play—holiday time, the Nadam.

The Nadam has little changed since the great days of the Mongol Empire. No longer does the Golden Horde hold sway from Budapest to the Great Wall. No longer does a Mogul rule India, and long since the Khans have been driven from golden Kazan. But the Nadam has survived almost unchanged. The three great "games of men" go on: archery, wrestling and horse racing. The competitions follow rigid rules laid down hundreds of years ago.

Today Mongolia is a Communist state ruled by Communist leaders, adhering to a Marxist philosophy, guided by the dialectic. But the Nadam is held in early July, as it was under Genghis Khan.

There are changes, of course. In addition to the archery and the traditional wrestling with its ritual analogies to eagles, lions and elephants, there is a great parade through the central square, a duplicate on a smaller scale of the November 7 procession in Moscow.

Some time during the night of July 11–12, 1966, in Ulan Bator, Mongolia's capital, we heard the rain begin to beat on the windows of our hotel. It was still falling at 6 A.M. when loudspeakers in Sukhe Bator Square, in the heart of the city, awakened us with the national anthem, proclaiming the start of the holiday. It continued to rain. It rained as we watched truckload after truckload of young people and children gathering for the march past. It poured down on infantry units and artillery, lumbering tanks and gun carriages assembled in the streets leading into the square. It turned to soggy pulp the banners celebrating achievements of the coal miners, the textile weavers, the shoe factory workers and the sheep herders. The dye from the artificial flowers carried by the children washed into pools of red and blue and yellow in the pavement.

But the holiday went forward. Youngsters in T-shirts, girls in thin blue blouses, danced and trotted double time in their places trying to keep warm in the driving downpour.

Promptly at 9 A.M. we saw the parade begin with the thunder of salute guns. Huddled under umbrellas, Ulan Bator's little diplomatic corps watched the Mongol troops slog by. Despite the downpour they recorded one impressive fact. Last year the feature of the parade was the camels. This year there were no camels. There were missiles.

For months I had heard rumors of the presence of Soviet missiles in Mongolia. Now the fact was confirmed. The missiles were evidence of mounting military concern over the long border with China. Mongolia has 2,670 miles of frontier with China, most of it vast desert wastes or wilderness mountain ranges. Soviet strategic concern over these open approaches from China provided a reliable index of tensions between Moscow and Peking.

The first time I visited Mongolia in 1959 I found Russia and China openly competing for supremacy. Mongolia, since shortly before World War I, had been a ward of Russia. First, Imperial Russia had assumed that role. Then Lenin's Russia continued it by assisting in the establishment of a Communist regime in Ulan Bator in 1921. For several hundreds of years before 1913 China had played the dominant role in Mongolia, and in 1959 Peking was making a strenuous bid to resume that position.

China had never really acquiesced in Russia's paramount position in Mongolia. She was too weak to prevent the czarist intrigue of 1913, just as Chiang Kai-shek was too weak in 1945 to prevent Stalin from reasserting the Russian position. Later Chiang repudiated his reluctant acquiescence. Mao nominally conceded Mongolia's independence. But in 1959 the Chinese were trying to woo Mongolia to their side again. It was the opening phase of the Sino-Soviet split, about which—at that time—the Western world was still oblivious until the evidence I gathered on the scene was published.

In 1959 China had allies in Mongolia. There were many Mongols who hinted to me that they hoped to play China against Russia and win for their country greater freedom of action. There were many Mongols who hoped that they might somehow be able to create a Greater Mongolia which would draw together all the Mongols—the 900,000 in Mongolia itself, the 1,500,000 in Inner Mongolia (ruled by China) and the 500,000 in Buryat-Mongolia (ruled by Russia).

I visited Mongolia again in 1961. Only two years had passed, but great changes had occurred. The Sino-Soviet split was public knowledge by now. And the Russians in Mongolia were driving hard to nail down their position. There had been possibly forty thousand Chinese workers in Mongolia in 1959. Now they numbered less than ten thousand, and they lived behind barbed wire in barracks, forbidden any contact with the Mongols. The Russians had been pouring in foreign aid funds, and it seemed clear to me that they had the Chinese on the run.

In 1966 I quickly saw that things had gone much further. The Russians had won the game. They had ended, for the time being, the hope of the Chinese that they might pull Mongolia over to their side.

The missiles were evidence of the seriousness with which the Soviet took the Chinese threat. But they were only part of the story.

The Russians put aid funds into Mongolia at a rate which made the Chinese contributions look piddling. The new Soviet aid agreement covering the 1966–70 period provided 660 million rubles—$720 million, a sum equal to nearly $700 a head for the 1.1 million Mongols. This came on top of an almost equal total in the five years previous.

In addition, Moscow had persuaded Czechoslovakia, Poland, East Germany and Bulgaria (among others) to provide Mongolia with technical assistance. It seemed to me that the Mongols were being smothered in aid to the extent that their economy was badly distorted. Ulan Bator, the capital of the country, had swelled to a population of 260,000—up nearly 100 percent in eight years. A quarter of Mongolia's scanty populace was now concentrated here. Despite enormous building programs, I estimated as we drove about the city that 60 percent of the dwellers still lived in yurts, an unhealthy, inconvenient, unsanitary way of urban life. The tempo of development was sucking into the capital workers badly needed in rural areas and complicating economic progress rather than assisting it. On a smaller scale, the Soviet by its excessive spending was creating exactly the kind of socioeconomic problem produced by similar U.S. programs in other backward Asian lands.

But Moscow was prepared to take no chances with Mongolia. Not only was the money pouring in. The Mongol Communist Party was being purged of every element which might be a source of unreliability.

This produced the greatest purge of the Mongolian Party in its history—and it had, I knew, undergone severe ones. In the last five years 83 of the 147 members of the Central and Revision committees had been changed. Nine of eighteen regional secretaries had been replaced. The whole Party had suffered a 41 percent turnover in membership. Most of this occurred in connection with a crisis in December, 1964, when a group of top-ranking elements in the Party was dismissed on charges of "nationalist chauvinism"—a euphemism for possible sympathy with the Chinese.

Premier Yumzhagin Tsedenbal shuttled back and forth between

Ulan Bator and Moscow in the special Tu-104 jet transport which had been presented to him by the Soviet Government. He made the trip in seven hours. I knew of no other leader in the Communist world who had concentrated more power into his hands than he in the years since he took over after the death of Choibalsan in 1952. Certainly no leader of a small Communist country could boast having gotten more for his country. But the largess was an embarrassment, and he was forced to tell the 15th Party Congress early in 1966 that the pace of investment in industry must be cut back.

The rise of Soviet concern over the military situation in Mongolia became more and more marked in 1966. The year began with a visit to Ulan Bator of Leonid Brezhnev, the Soviet Party Secretary. Accompanied by Foreign Minister Gromyko and Defense Minister Marshal Rodion Y. Malinovsky, he came to Mongolia to sign a new twenty-year treaty of cooperation, friendship and mutual assistance.

The new treaty provided that the Soviet Union not only would assist Mongolia's defense in event of attack but that the two signatories would take "all necessary steps, including military steps, to ensure the security, independence and territorial integrity of the two countries."

Malinovsky inspected Mongolian frontier defenses. His visit was followed by a succession of Soviet missions.

Had the Soviet Union put troops into Mongolia? I could find no diplomat in Ulan Bator who knew the answer. Soviet troops had been stationed in Mongolia almost continuously since 1921. They were there in large numbers in the years through the end of World War II, when the Soviet was on guard against Japanese attack (and, indeed, fought an undeclared war on the Mongol frontier at Khalkin Gal). I had heard persistent rumors that one or more Soviet divisions had been stationed in eastern Mongolia in the area of the industrial center of Choibalsan, close to China. But I could get no confirmation in Mongolia. Diplomats had been unable to get permission to visit Choibalsan. They had not seen Soviet combat troops themselves.

The Lo Wu railroad station. Here more than 450,000 persons a year cross into China; somewhat more than that number emerge.

Cambodia's lush and beautiful rice fields.

On the Cambodian-Vietnam frontier, Cambodian troops show where U.S. shells splintered jungle trees.

Gangtok (capital of Sikkim) through the eternal fog.

Angkor Wat, Cambodia.

Apsaras, the heavenly dancers of Cambodian mythology, from the frieze at Angkor Wat.

Bangkok's famous floating market.

Shopper goes to market
on Bangkok *klong* or canal.

Another Bangkok shopper.

Kaung Hmudaw Pagoda
in Pagan, Burma.
Designed after the breast
of the King's favorite wife.

Above, India's population problem, village children; below, Tibetan refugees.

Above, Sikkim ceremonial greeting for Gyalmo, the former Hope Cooke; below, Gyalmo, son Palden, Chogyal.

Central square, Khabarovsk.

Amur River, Khabarovsk. Czarist fort to right on river bank.

Lake Baikal.

Harbor at Nakhodka.

Sukhe Bator Square, Ulan Bator.

Mrs. Chester Bowles
and author
visiting Indian village.

The presence of missiles in the hands of the Mongol Army, however, suggested to me that Soviet training missions were assisting the Mongols in mastering the new techniques. Soviet construction troops were at work in Darkhan, to the north of Ulan Bator, an industrial site being developed with Soviet, Czech and Bulgarian assistance. And in Ulan Bator itself there was a detachment of four thousand Soviet Army engineers, building apartment houses, constructing roads and bridges.

Was it simple coincidence that the Soviet troops worked in the south end of town while in the north end there was an equal force of Chinese, precisely four thousand construction workers, engaged in a similar task? I did not think so.

When I had watched the Nadam parade in 1959, the Chinese marched in it, wearing their blue blouses, their blue trousers and their blue caps. They carried blue parasols, and I knew, from watching their early-morning setting-up exercises, that they wore blue undershirts. They were blue ants. The description was apt.

The Chinese did not march in the 1966 Nadam parade. We had seen them hard at work the day before, even though it was a Sunday, a free day in Ulan Bator. They were busy in the apartment buildings they were erecting alongside the Tola River, which flowed through the center of town. I could not but wonder whether they worked all through the opening day of Nadam as well, despite the rain.

The rain by midday of the Nadam opening had become a phenomenon. It was pouring down in endless sheets. The government tried to carry on with the holiday. The games were due to open with an athletic parade in the stadium at 1 P.M. The games were opened, but the parade had to be postponed to the next day. The rains went on. That evening the government held its great diplomatic reception. The vodka flowed so freely that it was difficult to determine whether it was wetter inside the Government Palace or outside. But as guests left the great hall on the distant side of the Tola River, they were alarmed to see the river boiling up almost to the level of the bridges. The rain continued.

In the morning we awakened to find it was still raining. Later on we were to learn that in the first twenty-four hours one-third of Ulan Bator's average annual rainfall had poured down—98.5 millimeters. By noon the next day the Tola River had reached a height of 311 centimeters—more than twice the previous record of 151 centimeters.

The Tola, normally a stone-and-boulder-bedded stream less than one hundred feet wide, now began to fan out to one hundred yards, two hundred yards, a quarter-mile, a half-mile. The whole center of the city was being engulfed.

The rain halted at noon on Tuesday. At midafternoon Charlotte and I walked down through the main street of town to the Peace Bridge, the large bridge connecting the two sides of the city. As we made our way along the street, streams of refugees and citizens came toward us. The city was in the throes of an advancing disaster. The waters swirled around the foundations of the bridge. Already the other bridges to the south had gone out. We saw the telltale white domes of yurts disappearing in the flood and the churning of debris. As far as the eye could see, the heart of the city was going under water. But as we walked past the Chinese building encampment, we heard the hammer of Chinese carpenters, the whir of the Chinese donkey engines, the buzz of Chinese saws. It was Mongolia's national holiday. It was a day of Mongol disaster. To the Chinese it was just another working day.

Not for the Russians. Soon we heard the racket of helicopters and saw lines of army trucks moving toward the disaster areas. These were Russian helicopters, Russian trucks. The Soviet Army construction battalions were rushing to the rescue.

But not the Chinese. The Chinese made no secret of their disdain for and contempt of the Mongols. At a Bastille Day reception of the new French Ambassador the Chinese Ambassador sneered at the difficulties. In China, he said, nothing like this would have happened. And if it had happened it would have been quickly taken in hand. It was true, of course, that the Mongol Government, preoccupied with its holiday, had not been quick off the mark at realizing disaster was in the making. Even if it had, the magnitude of the flood would have made emergency measures of dubious value.

Regardless of responsibility, the problem now was first aid, urgent assistance, rescue work. Day and night we watched the Russians and hastily mobilized Mongols struggled with the flood waters. Helicopters and trucks turned the vast acreage of Sukhe Bator Square just a block from our hotel into a rescue depot. Hundreds of families, their sodden possessions and their frightened children were trucked to the square to await movement to emergency camps. New yurt colonies sprouted on the green hills around Ulan Bator. Thousands of persons who lived on the low-lying banks of the Tola had lost their tents and all their possessions. Many had lost their children as well. For the toll among young children was highest. Russian and Mongolian amphibious trucks, ducks and landing craft plunged into the swirling waters to save marooned families.

The festivities of Nadam were abandoned. The flood had submerged Ulan Bator's water pumping station. It had knocked out the power plant and left our hotel without water, toilet facilities and light. We went for a week without baths and ate cold meals from an army field kitchen. The flood swamped almost every factory in the city and cut off access to great blocks of living areas. There was no light, no power, no water, no heat. The sewer system did not work. Food depots were flooded. Only one bakery still functioned. The railroad to Russia on the north was cut. The railroad to China on the south was cut in four places where bridges and long stretches of the embankment were washed out. The airport was isolated by the flooding of the road along the river. It was the worst natural catastrophe the country had suffered in modern times.

This was the situation which brought sneers to the face of the Chinese Ambassador. When the Mongolian Government called in the diplomatic corps, gave it the facts of the disaster and announced that it would welcome aid of any kind, it was the Russians and the East European Communist countries which hurried to help. West European countries made offers of aid. Even the United States offered a small grant. From the Chinese side there was silence. Nothing could have more eloquently emphasized the complete abandonment of the struggle for Mongolian partisanship by the Chinese.

For practical purposes contacts between Mongolia and China had virtually ended. When I first visited Mongolia in 1959, there was direct airplane service from Moscow to Ulan Bator by two lines—the Soviet Aeroflot and the Chinese line. The great Tu-104's flew on regular twice-a-week runs with a changeover in Irkutsk to smaller planes (the Ulan Bator airport could not handle the big jets). From Irkutsk there were three weekly planes—one Soviet, one Mongol, one Chinese. I flew the Chinese plane. There was the same service to Peking—three planes a week, one of each country. There was daily rail service between Ulan Bator and Peking on the direct line which had been completed in 1956. There was a curious feature about this line. It was built across Mongolia to the wide Russian gauge. This wide track was continued into China for more than sixty miles to the city of Tsining. The Chinese line and gauge came to this city.

Here, deep within China, was the transit point for freight and passengers bound from Mongolia or Russia into China.

Now all this had been changed. The elaborate plane services to Peking had been eliminated. No longer did the Chinese jet fly to Moscow. In fact, there was no plane service from Ulan Bator to Peking. If a diplomat in Ulan Bator wanted to go to Peking, he had to fly to the Soviet city of Irkutsk and there catch the sole weekly Soviet plane which flew to the Chinese capital.

Rail service had been curtailed. The wide-gauge tracks had been torn up and relaid in Chinese gauge right up to the Mongol frontier town of Dzamyn Ude. Not only had the track been torn up; all traffic to and from China virtually had ended. Premier Tsedenbal admitted to the 15th Party Congress that transit freight had fallen to one-eighth its previous level, bringing down the over-all volume of rail freight to a point at which the Mongol railroads suffered serious operational and financial difficulties.

The great Nadam flood completed China's isolation from Mongolia. Rail service was suspended completely. While the Soviet rushed in special crews and quickly restored the northern branch of the trans-Mongol line, repairs to the Mongol-China link got the lowest kind of priority. Neither the Mongols nor the Russians cared how long the link was out of service. If the Chinese had any concern, they concealed it magnificently. Months later the railroad still had not been put back into service.

Contact between Mongolia and Tibet had come to an end as early as 1959. Now ties between Mongolia and Inner Mongolia followed the same course. The Chinese had attempted to play on Mongol nationalistic sensibilities by sponsoring elaborate observance of the eight hundredth anniversary of Genghis Khan. It was an attractive gambit. Genghis Khan is the hero of all Mongols. His is the only Mongol name known the world over. Regardless of politics, Mongols venerate the man who once made the earth tremble at his approach. Russians do not. Their memories of the Mongol invasion, the nearly three hundred years when they were held in thrall under the Mongol *yarlik*, are bitter. When Mongol writers hailed the anniversary, they were savagely attacked by Moscow as chauvinists, as purveyors of an anti-Russian, anti-Marxist line.

Cultural contacts between the Mongols of Inner and Outer Mongolia ground to a complete halt. A small Mongol group visited Peking in the spring of 1966, but, I was told, they did not meet with their Inner Mongol compatriots. In contrast, contact between Mongols and the Buryat-Mongols of the Soviet Union—held at arm's length by the Russians for some years—became more frequent.

Tibet continued as sealed to Mongols as to all other outsiders. But to Mongolia this action had deeper significance. Tibet was

Mongolia's spiritual home, the source of its Buddhist religion, the goal of Mongol pilgrimage for countless centuries. More keenly than other peoples the Mongols felt the barrier which was dropped around Tibet by the Chinese.

Mongolia, I felt certain, had firmly cast its lot with the Soviet Union. And yet that was not the whole story. The Mongols dreamed of a more independent role in the world, of a role in which they would have more real initiative, in which they would be less tied to either of their great neighbors. For nearly a decade Mongolia had been moving slowly, cautiously, persistently in this direction. They had won their long fight for membership in the United Nations. They had begun to play host to an occasional international conference, including one on women's rights, sponsored by the UN. They had begun to broaden their area of diplomatic contact. Two major Western powers—Britain and France—now maintained fully accredited missions in Ulan Bator. The total of countries with which Mongolia had diplomatic relations was approaching forty. Mongolia was striving to widen her foreign trade base, particularly with countries like West Germany, France, Britain and Japan. If the volume had not yet reached notable totals, this was due more to lack of trading goods than anything else.

But Mongolia was still blocked in one of the chief goals of her foreign policy—the establishment of relations with the United States. Washington in the summer of 1962 had come to the point of recognizing Mongolia. But at the last moment we had backed away in fear of complicated reprisals by the Chinese Nationalist Government. After a four-year interval the United States began again to move toward a new initiative. But this ran aground on the rocks of the Vietnam war. In the harsh atmosphere between East and West generated by the Viet conflict Ulan Bator felt its hands tied. Much as it desired contact with the United States, important as American relations were in the context of Mongolia's effort to move out into the world, the Mongols told me they did not see that their way would be clear to go forward so long as the Vietnam conflict remained unresolved.

Would Mongolia stay firmly lodged in the Soviet camp? I did not think events had left Mongolia much freedom of maneuver. So long as the Soviet-Chinese struggle continued, Mongolia was deprived of ability to shift her weight. Yet I could not help pondering one symbolic fact. There were in Ulan Bator two statues of Stalin—two of the few that survive in that part of the Communist world which looked to Moscow for leadership. No such statues still stood in Poland, Czechoslovakia, Rumania and Hungary. If any remained in Bulgaria, they were well hidden. True, Stalin still looked down on Tirana's central square. But Albania was Moscow's fiercest Communist foe. Stalin portraits were held aloft by Red Guard demonstrators outside the Soviet Embassy in Peking and Stalin posters were borne through the great square in Peking during the Chinese parades.

But in all the Soviet Union there were no statues of Stalin except for three or four which survived in Georgia, Stalin's birthplace.

The two statues in Ulan Bator were not inconspicuous. One stood in front of the Academy of Science building, in the heart of the city, on the main street, only a block from the Sukhe Bator Square. It was the first thing to strike Charlotte's eye as we drove into the capital from the airport. The other statue was outside the Ulan Bator University. I well remembered that in 1959 Stalin portraits were still hung up for the Mongol holidays.

Nothing in a Communist country is accidental, certainly nothing so political as the statue of Stalin. Why did Stalin's statues still stand in Ulan Bator? Was their presence, perhaps, a silent but visible reminder to the Russians that, whatever their massive aid, whatever their military commitment, whatever Mongolia's political alignment, there did exist an alternative way? The Stalin statues were never mentioned. Mongols never gave them a second glance. But no Russian could arrive in Mongolia without being rocked by them.

Throughout the Communist world, it was my observation that no force was more powerful than that of nationalism. It had been the propellant which moved Yugoslavia out of Moscow's orbit. It had done the same with Albania. It underlay the Soviet difficulties in

Poland and Hungary in 1956 and the troubles with Rumania in 1966. It was at the core of the Soviet-Chinese dispute.

I left Mongolia in the summer of 1966 convinced that firm as Tsedenbal was in his friendship with Moscow, strong as Mongolia's sympathies lay with Russia, there would always be another chapter opening in the ceaseless drive of Mongolia for full unity, full independence. The Chinese might sneer today. But they were a patient people. They had seen many changes in Mongolia over the hundreds of years. The next turn might well bring the Mongols back toward the East.

Meantime, each side bided its time. The frontiers of Mongolia were well guarded. There had been clashes between Mongols and Chinese, between Russians and Chinese. There might be new clashes and skirmishes at any moment, even major undeclared wars, in the pattern of those fought between Russia and Japan in the 1930's.

The last cards in the game of the Mongols, the Russians and the Chinese were yet to be played.

And there might one day be a fourth player in that game. One evening I heard the strains of a familiar song blaring out in the lobby of the Ulan Bator Hotel. The lobby was filled with important delegates assembled from all ends of the Communist world for the Nadam holiday—Russians, Hungarians, Poles, Czechs, North Vietnamese, possibly even a Chinese or two. I listened to the music as I walked down the broad staircase. It certainly was familiar. "Downtown," a girl's voice echoed, "everything's better downtown. . . ." There was no mistaking the faintly nasal, faintly nostalgic tones of Petula Clark. At the far end of the lobby a cluster of young Mongols had gathered around a record player, listening to the song which had sold hundreds of thousands of copies in England and America. Petula Clark was not the only star of the Western world to capture the fancy of the Mongols. Nor was it only Mongol youth that was enthralled. Two American jukeboxes had been especially imported from East Berlin to provide music for the Nadam. One of the gleaming Rowe-AMI machines was set up in the main dining room of the Ulan Bator Hotel, the other in the special private dining room for VIP delegations. Each had one hundred selections. None were Russian, none were Chinese and, naturally, none were Mongol.

There were more Petula Clark numbers. There were Glenn Miller's "Red Roses for a Blue Lady," two or three Beatles numbers, Dean Martin in "Bumming Around," Frank Sinatra in "I Can't Believe It," the Animals, Elvis Presley, the Yardbirds and the Rolling Stones.

The young Mongols who gathered in awe around these dazzling examples of Western culture wore boxy hip-length knit sweaters, Oliver Twist caps, skin-tight trousers, miniskirts, and Italian pointed soft-leather shoes. They had abandoned the flowing silk *del* and the culture of the yurt for the mode of the mods. They were switched on. Given a chance, it seemed clear to me, the new generation of Mongolia would turn its back on both Peking's orthodoxy and Moscow's new eclecticism. They might not yet be ready for LBJ's "Great Society," but the ways of the mod certainly would win any "Great Cultural Revolution" which took place in the ancient land of Genghis Khan.

10

Any Letters from Peking?

THE CUSTOMS OFFICIAL AT THE IRKUTSK AIRPORT WAS A PLEASANT thirty-year-old blonde with hazel eyes and an easy smile. She approached the row of five bags with a shake of her head.

"Open this one," she said, pointing to my attaché case.

She glanced at the bulging papers in the case, most of them materials which I had picked up in Mongolia.

"Do you have any letters from Peking?" she asked. Then quickly corrected herself. "I mean any letters from Ulan Bator. Any literature? Any manuscripts?"

The attaché case was filled with literature, not to mention a manuscript or two. In fact, she was holding some of these papers in her hands. But I understood perfectly what she meant. It was not letters, literature or manuscripts from Ulan Bator. It was propaganda from Peking against which she was on guard.

"No," I responded. "We've just been to Ulan Bator for the holiday, for the Nadam. I have no letters or literature."

She smiled and turned to a fellow inspector. "No need to look any further," she said. "They have nothing of interest to us."

I have been traveling across the Soviet frontier crossing point at Irkutsk for some years, in and out of Mongolia. The first time I went through, there were special facilities for Chinese officials and tourists. The principal traffic then was Chinese going to and

122

from the Soviet Union, and Soviet specialists going to and from China.

There were special waiting rooms, special dining rooms, special personnel to handle the Chinese traffic. I flew from Irkutsk to Ulan Bator in 1959 on a Chinese plane with Chinese passengers. I was the object of stares and suspicion. The Chinese got honored treatment. Even so, border control was close and careful. Five years before, when I had first traveled to eastern Siberia, one of the great surprises had been the security precautions which the Russians continued to maintain. I had been amazed in 1954 to find that all along the Trans-Siberian Railroad the military were much in evidence. Chita, headquarters for major forces of the Red Banner Far Eastern Army in the 1930's, was still a garrison town. Its forces were as large as or larger than when it stood guard against the Japanese. The presence of Soviet troops in large numbers from Irkutsk and the Baikal area onward to the east made a vivid impression.

What struck me so forcibly was that no longer did Russia possess a hostile neighbor in the Far East. Japan had long since vanished as a military power. Since 1949 the region south of the Amur had been occupied by Russia's close ally, Communist China. Why, then, did the Soviet maintain her garrisons in eastern Siberia at full strength?

There was no answer to the question in 1954. No hint of rift between Moscow and Peking had been permitted to show through the Iron or Bamboo curtains. But by 1959 things were beginning to change. The tensions had begun to show through, and one sign of those tensions was strict controls along the Soviet-Chinese frontier. By 1961, when I again visited eastern Siberia, security had become the watchword. Chinese moving in or out of Russia were subjected to cross-examination. Their baggage was turned inside out, and they were compelled to turn out their pockets and surrender their briefcases.

Now in 1966 the Soviet guard was up higher than ever.

I saw evidence of heightened vigilance from one end of Siberia to the other. The facilities of Siberian airports had been sharply improved. Gone were the old tar-surfaced or tamped-gravel runways. All the way East the concrete runways were broad and long and crisscrossed to take heavy jet traffic. Even the obscure Ulan Bator airport, with not more than a dozen scheduled major flights a week, now had jet runways capable of handling landings from any direction.

I had begun to notice these signs on our flight out of Moscow to Irkutsk and Ulan Bator the previous week. We had left Moscow at midevening of an early July night. As we flew across Siberia the sun's red glowed on the northern horizon. No real darkness exists in Siberia at that season. When we came down for a landing at Omsk in the cool early-morning light and taxied along the endless concrete strip, we passed through a small forest of aircraft. These were the enormous Tu-104 and Tu-114 long-range transports capable of carrying 150 persons at six hundred miles an hour. They had been stacked up on every airport in Siberia—enough, it seemed, to carry the Soviet Army to the ends of Asia, in case of emergency. So many aircraft were parked at the airports that the bays and coves could not handle them all. Instead, in grassy village streets, lined with peasant izbas, you could see the rear assemblies of the transports protruding high in the air like the tails of great firebirds.

A few years ago most Russian airports were mixed civil-military bases. Now, except for the stack-ups of jet transports, military aircraft operated from their own parallel bases. This seemed to be true of all the cities which are normally "open"—cities on the regular tourist or business routes across the Soviet Union.

But off the main routes the situation was different, as I later discovered when chance diverted our aircraft from Khabarovsk to Vladivostok, the great Russian Far Eastern naval base, closed to foreign travel for almost fifteen years. Some foreign shipping enters the port, but visits by tourists, diplomats and correspondents have been banned, presumably for security reasons. Perhaps that is why, as our Aeroflot Ilyushin-18 hurtled down the Vladivostok landing strip, we flashed by squadron after squadron of needle-nosed MIG-21's and MIG-19's—sixty or more in squadrons flanking the runway, ready for instant take-off to the south.

I have been traveling to eastern Siberia since the end of the Stalin era. It would not be accurate to report that the atmosphere in the summer of 1966 was tense. On Lake Baikal we watched the fishing boats ply their way as they had for two or three hundred years. Tourists flocked to the resorts on the volcanic hills which rise so steeply from the incredible blue waters of the mile-deep lake. High on a jutting shoulder above the Baikal Limnological Institute young men and girls played volleyball on a paved court just beside the "Eisenhower dacha"—the beautiful villa built for President Eisenhower to occupy on his trip to Russia in 1960, the ill-fated journey which he did not take because of the U-2 incident. Now the villa was used for other distinguished visitors and around it had grown up a pleasant resort. "Someday, perhaps," a young man said at Baikal, "President Eisenhower, or some other President, may yet pay us a visit. But not President Johnson, I think."

The echoes of the outer world, the tensions between Moscow and Peking, the tensions over Vietnam did not press hard on eastern Siberia. But they could be felt.

"No," an Irkutsk woman said, "we don't see many Chinese any more. There was a group of young Chinese here in early summer. They were members of a youth organization on a tour. They were well behaved. For once, there were no incidents. But they are strange people. Difficult to understand."

She said that three or four years ago, before the Chinese stopped coming almost entirely, there had been difficult times with Chinese visitors. "They have very pronounced opinions," she said. "They insist on one thing or another and there is no way to argue with them."

Irkutsk was more concerned about a subject close to home— pollution of Lake Baikal. On the south shore of the lake, close to the heavily timbered regions, the Soviet Paper Trust was erecting one of the largest pulp mills in the world. The plant was scheduled for completion in 1966 or early in 1967. It would discharge billions of gallons of raw sulphuric wastes into Baikal.

Baikal possesses a unique ecology. It is the world's largest fresh-water body—water of unbelievable purity. the closest thing in nature to distilled water. The lake is so large that if all the rivers of the world were turned into it, it would take 230 days to fill. It could hold all the American Great Lakes. Once polluted, it will require more than four hundred years to rid it of pollution—that is the time it would take the 336 rivers which pour into it to replace the water now there.

"You can see why we are concerned over the pulp mill," a young scientist said at the Limnological Institute. I told him the whole world was aware of the threat to Baikal and that conservationists in the United States had joined in the appeal to Soviet authorities to prevent the despoliation. I mentioned the publicity given to a speech by Mikhail Sholokhov, the author of *Quiet Flows the Don*, in which he attacked the plans for ravishing Baikal.

"Yes," the young man said. "We know of the interest. And, of course, we were glad to hear Sholokhov speak. Especially since he has never even bothered to visit Siberia or see Lake Baikal."

The scientist said that a proposal had been made to the Soviet Government to build a giant pipeline around the south end of Baikal to carry the sulphite wastes to the Angara River, thus by-passing Lake Baikal.

"But," the young man sadly said, "that would cost millions of rubles. The Paper Trust is interested in production and profits. So far no one seems willing to spend the money to prevent this crime."

No other environment in the world matches that of Baikal. The lake is about twenty million years old. The site was once volcanic and suffers occasional earth tremors. It is essentially an enormous mountain range of which only the tips are exposed, trapping tre-mendous quantities of fresh water in its sheer valleys. It is four hundred miles long and sixty miles across at the widest point, divided by submerged mountain ridges into three sections, each with its own kind of plant and marine life. Its greatest depth is about 5,800 feet. More than one thousand kinds of animals and fish and five hundred species of plants are found in Baikal—70 percent of them not duplicated anywhere else in the world. Here is the home of the *nerpa*, the world's only fresh-water seal. Here is a remarkable range of wild mink—a breed so powerful and active that they often bring down a deer or an elk by leaping from an overhanging limb and slashing the animal's jugular vein. The pride of Baikal is the *omul*, a delicate and tender fish somewhat like a lake trout. There are three hundred kinds of crayfish in the lake, some living at a depth of nine hundred feet and possessing a translucent, almost transparent, bone structure.

All this is threatened by the profit-hungry Soviet Paper Trust.

Two thousand miles to the east, in Khabarovsk-on-the-Amur, the China question loomed larger, darker—almost as large and dark as the thunderheads which studded the horizon as we flew above the Ussuri River which marks the Chinese-Soviet boundary between Vladivostok and Khabarovsk. The thunderheads snapped and crackled with inner lightning which discharged like the sudden molten flare of a blast furnace's spill. The pilot of the Il-18 dodged and twisted to avoid the black clouds and the great sparks. He was driven again and again to the west, closer and closer to the Ussuri, which lay twisting and turning, its course dimly illuminated by the unearthly discharges. Beyond the Ussuri dark mountains loomed in the velvet dusk. This was China. To the one side pressed the thunderheads, to the other the dark mass of China. To the pilot it was Scylla and Charybdis. Were there antiaircraft batteries mounted in the brooding mountains? Where lay the greatest danger, in the thunderheads which threatened at any moment to twist our plane into crumpled metal or in the hidden guns beyond the frontier? I could not read the pilot's calculations, but I sensed from the desperation with which he dove and twisted toward each corridor between the lightning-laden clouds that he preferred the terrible danger he could see to the one which might lurk in the Chinese mountains. We did not cross the frontier, but at moments we skirted perilously near.

The China threat seems close in Khabarovsk because China is close. Charlotte and I stood on the concrete embankment along the Amur. On a bluff above us was the old palace of the czarist governor general, now a theater and dramatic institute. Beyond were the turrets of one of the first stone Russian forts along the Amur. A spanking wind stirred the river into angry waves and forced us to forego a boat trip down the bend "toward China."

"Across the river and over those mountains is China," a Soviet official said. "The Chinese call this the Black Dragon River. Did you know that?"

"And are there black dragons beyond the mountains?" I asked.

"What do you think?" the Russian replied. "But we're on guard against them. Just let them try something."

I had last been in Khabarovsk in 1954. In those times it was still the headquarters of the Soviet secret police administration which ran most of eastern Siberia as a forced labor camp. From this grim city were directed the terrible gold mining camps of Kolyma, the timber industries of the Maritimes, the transport lines which linked together the desolate empire once bossed by the dread chief of Secret Police, Lavrenti P. Beriya. The largest building in Khabarovsk then was the Interior Ministry headquarters. Nowhere in Russia were the police activities more blatant, more open. There were three forced-labor construction sites on the main street of the city, each with its tommy gunners, its barbed wire, its watchtowers. Nowhere in Russia, and on no occasion, had I so strongly felt the omnipresence of the police. Khabarovsk was the true capital of a police empire.

Not so today. The city bustled with prosperity. It had grown vastly, doubling in size under the beneficent policy of the Khrushchev and Kosygin-Brezhnev regimes. Gone were the ubiquitous blue-and-red caps of the security police. Security headquarters was still there, but it seemed to me no more busy than any government bureau. Outside the city had grown up new industrial suburbs, colonies of summer cottages. Khabarovsk was in the throes of a modest boom. True, I did meet residents who had settled there in exile or who had stayed on after some Stalinist years in a concentration camp. But the police atmosphere had gone. In its place was a military presence. It reminded me of Chita a dozen years before. The army was the biggest thing in Khabarovsk. Its uniforms were everywhere on the main streets, in the shops, in the restaurants and public buildings. The Officers Club was a splendid big building. The army sports center and stadium was the finest east of Moscow. Khabarovsk had become the headquarters of the Soviet command to defend the Far East against Chinese encroachments.

And this was a matter for the present, not the future. For there had already been encroachments. In the West I had heard discussions as to what lay behind China's territorial demands against Russia. Were they real? Was it all propaganda? Were the Chinese preparing to back their demands with force?

Along the Amur, I found, the Chinese were taken seriously. No one thought that China was simply making headlines when she said that of the nine unequal treaties under which territory had been taken from China three were imposed by Russia. No one thought it mere braggadocio that China had staked a claim to the Amur River area on which Khabarovsk stood—along with the bulk of eastern Siberia west to Baikal and east to Vladivostok. No one thought China was joking in her attack on the Soviet position in Mongolia. No one thought that China was joking in her suggestion that half of Soviet Central Asia was rightfully hers.

The reason for this was simple. Already along the Amur armed clashes had occurred. Already on the Amur, Soviet and Chinese forces had fought. The conflicts were small, almost trivial, but the precedent had been laid. The Chinese had seized several islands in the Amur which the Russians had long occupied. They had stated their claim to all the other Amur islands. They had gone further. They had laid the groundwork for imposing Chinese control on all the waterways to which they asserted title—the Amur, the Ussuri and Lake Khanka—almost seven thousand miles of navigable waterways.

Ever since 1949 the Russians and the Chinese had been jointly sharing these watercourses. They signed an agreement in 1962 guaranteeing the free movement of shipping along contiguous waterways and into connecting streams.

Then on April 19, 1966, I discovered, the Chinese had published regulations governing foreign ships on frontier rivers. They were directed, obviously, at the Russians. No other "foreign" ships use the waters. They imposed on Soviet shipping a system of permits, compulsory pilots and inspections. No photographs may be taken by crewmen. No drawings may be made. The crews may not go fishing or swimming. They may not sound the rivers, moor or debark except at Chinese sufferance. The Soviet captains must report any weapons, ammunition, wireless transmitters, radar equipment, signal rockets or signal guns which they are carrying. They must turn over all weapons and ammunition to the Chinese Harbor Supervision Office. They are barred from the use of wireless, radar or signal guns. They must hoist the Chinese flag on the foremast.

No effort had been made by late 1966 to enforce these regulations. But the Russians took them with utmost seriousness. Why should the Chinese publish the rules unless they planned, sooner or later, to enforce them?

The Russians were taking no chances. They had built up the strength of their river patrol forces. They had built up the strength of their major garrisons along the Amur. If the Chinese wanted a fight, they could have it. And in point of fact the Russians contended there had already been some hundreds of incidents.

Perhaps the most serious of these had occurred in one of the most remote areas of the world, the desert-and-mountain frontier which separated China's southwestern province of Sinkiang from the eastern reaches of the Soviet's Kazakhstan and Kirghizia. For nearly a century the Russians had had a foothold in Sinkiang—often more than a foothold. In the last czarist years Russia through trade and intrigue dominated this distant area. The same was true for decades under the Soviets. Soviet influence was paramount in western Sinkiang through the 1930's. It waned briefly in World War II, then came back strongly. There were times when Sinkiang was run from the Soviet consulate general's office in Urumchi and the Soviet military command in Ili (Kulja).

Western Sinkiang is inhabited not by Chinese but by nomadic Moslem peoples—Uigurs, Kazaks and Kirghiz, who have close ethnic and cultural connections with their cousins in the Soviet Union. Traditionally, they have moved with their animals freely across the dim and obscure frontiers, without interference from any authority. When I traveled there in the early post-Stalin years I met tribesmen from the Soviet side who found ready employment minding flocks on the China side, then came back to Russia to settle down or spend their earnings.

There had been large Russian colonies in Sinkiang from czarist times. The Russian numbers increased at the time of the Revolution and after, when many peasants fled into China to escape the terrors of Stalin's collectivization.

In the first flush of the Chinese Communist victory joint plans were elaborated by the Soviet and Chinese for development of the region. There were joint oil and mining ventures and an elaborate scheme for linking China's Sinkiang and Russia's Kazakhstan by rail. The development went by the board when the Chinese began to perceive that Stalin's idea of a joint venture was one in which he kept the control and the lion's share of the profits. Mao felt there wasn't much difference between Stalin's ideas and those of the "imperialist" British traders.

The railroad project did not die immediately. The Russians had only a short link to build. They ran a line 120 miles from Aktogai on the Turb-Sib Railroad to the Dungarian gates. There it was

§   *131*

supposed to meet a Chinese link coming west from Lanchow across Kansu to Urumchi, Sinkiang's capital, and then on to the Sino-Soviet frontier. The Chinese finished their line to Urumchi and continued about thirty miles farther west. But there they halted, and there they were still halted in 1966, about 250 miles short of the border. Meantime, they busied themselves building a line from Lake Kok Nor to Tibet.

Between forty and fifty thousand Uigurs and Kazaks had fled across the Sinkiang frontier into the Soviet Union in the past four or five years. There had been repeated armed clashes between Soviet frontier forces and Chinese. In mid-1966 the Soviet realigned its command in the border area, bringing in additional units. The Russians also formed special militia detachments of collective farmers and herdsmen in the remote areas to halt raids across the line by the Chinese.

The Chinese claimed that the unrest among minorities had been stimulated by the Russians—a charge which may have had some foundation in the light of the decades of Soviet activity in Sinkiang. But it was also true that the Chinese policy of enforced Sinofication aroused the antagonism of racial minorities. The Chinese persistently pursued a policy of settling Han (Chinese) in Sinkiang in order to shift the racial balance in their favor. In 1949 the province had a population of 3,750,000, of whom only 200,000 were Chinese. By 1962 the population was 7,000,000—nearly double—and Chinese numbered nearly 2,000,000. The Chinese total in 1966 was estimated at 2,500,000, more than one-third of the total.

The Russians may not have stimulated native opposition in Sinkiang. But they gave free access to any and all refugees, even permitting small groups of Uigurs to cross Soviet territory in order to pass into Afghanistan and the West.

The Chinese retaliated, I was told, by resolutely eliminating from Sinkiang all Russians. At the end of World War II there were between sixty and seventy thousand in Sinkiang out of a total of 200,000 Russians in China. Most of these Russians were émigrés

who left Russia at the time of the Bolshevik Revolution or there-
after. There were large White Russian colonies in Shanghai, Harbin,
Tientsin, Mukden. These colonies were rapidly liquidated in the late
1940's, many Russians being persuaded to return to the motherland
at the end of World War II and others leaving under Communist
Chinese pressure in 1949 and 1950.

The Russians in Sinkiang followed the same course. I had earlier
met some of them—for a tiny trickle was still coming out—in Hong
Kong. They estimated that possibly three hundred of their countrymen were still in Sinkiang and perhaps eight hundred in all of
China.

I asked Mikhail Haberlein, a Russian-born farmer whose father
emigrated from western Siberia to Kulja in Sinkiang before World
War I, why he had left. Haberlein was a Russian of Volga *Deutsch*
ancestry—his ancestors came to Russia at the time of Catherine II
and settled on the Volga. He, his Russian wife and four children
had suffered great hardships. His two brothers had died in Russian
concentration camps. He had been a prosperous miller and merchant
as well as a farmer. His possessions had been taken from him by
the Chinese (but they permitted him to continue to run his mill).

"The Chinese were quite friendly and polite," he said. "But
they kept coming to us and saying, 'Look here, you're a Russian—
what are you doing here? Why don't you go home?'"

Haberlein told them he didn't want to go to the Soviet Union.
He preferred to go to Germany. They kept at him.

They said: "You Russians are worse than all the other foreigners.
The British and French and Americans have all gone home. That
is where they belong. But you Russians are still here. You are
different from them. You settle on our land and stay."

Haberlein refused to go back to Russia. Finally, as the conflict
between China and Russia deepened, the Chinese took a new tack.
They would permit the Haberleins and the other Russians to go
to Hong Kong under United Nations auspices. It was this decision
which had brought several hundred Russians out of Sinkiang.

Haberlein hoped to go on to Germany. He had been in correspond-
ence with some distant relatives.

Ivan Neimtzov, a bearded Russian, a member of the sect of Old
Believers, also left Kulja in 1966. He had gone to China to escape
Stalin's collectivization drive. He liked it there. It was good farming
country, just like the country he had farmed in the region of
Semipalatinsk. He had no desire to leave, and he, too, refused to
return to Russia, despite Chinese arguments. The Chinese made it
harder and harder for him to farm. Taxes went up. There was always
some new restriction. The country grew unsettled. There was great
unrest among the Uigurs and the Kazaks. They did not like the
Chinese coming in and changing their way of life. Finally, Neimtzov
decided to take a chance and come out to Hong Kong. He was a
strong-minded man. The refugee authorities were trying to persuade
him to go to Australia. He had refused. He wanted to go to the
Argentine. Either that or he would just squat there in Hong Kong.

I asked him what it was like in Sinkiang.

"It used to be an area of strong Russian influence," he said.
"Now, it is not—for the time being."

As always in traveling across Siberia, I had the feeling of being
on familiar, friendly ground. Charlotte shared in this. No American
can fly over the endless pine and spruce forests, gaze on the blue
lakes, the crystal streams, breathe the fresh air, scent the fragrance
of the primroses, the goldenrod, the late lilacs (just blooming on
Lake Baikal in mid-July!), without sensing that here is a land he
knows and loves, the same land as the American West, the forests
of Montana, the blue streams of Colorado, the untouched loveliness
that was our West before the age of gasoline, rubber, concrete and
beer cans.

I felt again a kinship with the Siberian people—open, warm,
their minds bold and idiosyncratic. The old factory worker, exiled
to Siberia under Stalin, offered a chance to return to Moscow ten
years ago, rejecting the offer in scorn. He loves Siberia. Here he is
free. He wants no part of Moscow's stifling atmosphere. The Siberian

girl who shakes her dark head and says: "They were cowards not to publish Pasternak. We are old enough to read what we want and make up our own minds about it." The old Irkutsk man who snorts at the "monument to the three hundredth anniversary of Irkutsk" which stands outside the Irkutsk University. "What hypocrisy," he snaps. "That monument was erected to Alexander III. They took Alexander III down. It has never looked like anything since, and it never will." The girl who collects Beatle records but despises Beatle haircuts—particularly on Siberian boys. The Russian in Khabarovsk who listens to Radio Tokyo, BBC, Voice of America and Radio Peking. "Radio Tokyo is best," he says. "BBC isn't bad, but Radio Tokyo is more interesting. The Voice—well, it's better than it used to be. But it has a long way to go." What about Radio Peking? I ask him. "Oh, it had a big audience when it started to broadcast in Russian," he said. "The biggest. We all thought it was going to say something exciting. But now—well, we listen to it now and then, just in case. But it is so boring. It is worse than Radio Moscow."

What was really happening in China? I asked an intelligent Russian in eastern Siberia, a man who had concerned himself for fifteen years with questions of foreign affairs. Did he really think there was danger from Peking?

He thought a moment or two before replying.

"Look," he said. "We don't know what is happening in Peking. We don't know any more than you do. That is what is so frightening about it. We read what they say and we see what they do. What conclusion can we come to? The only thing I think is they must be crazy. Out of their minds. And that, you must admit, is a very dangerous thing. Maybe the most dangerous."

11
To the Pacific Ocean

THERE WAS A HOLIDAY ATMOSPHERE AS THE TRANS-SIBERIAN PULLED out of Khabarovsk station. Perhaps it was because the sign on the side of the *wagon-lits* simply read, "To the Pacific Ocean." Perhaps it was because this was the last segment of the long, long journey from Moscow. Most of our fellow passengers had already been traveling for seven days, and now they were filled with anticipation because soon the trip would end. Many were going on to Japan, including, of course, all the Japanese passengers.

The presence of the Japanese in Siberia first began to be borne in on me in Irkutsk. The hotel manager there was an old friend from past journeys. I asked whether the Chinese still came to Irkutsk. Not any more, she said. But many, many Japanese. "We have trouble in providing them with interpreters," she said. "They speak English—supposedly. But our girls can't understand them."

In Khabarovsk I felt the Japanese presence even stronger. There our guide was trilingual. He spoke Japanese as well as English. Most of the Intourist guides in Khabarovsk were Japanese-speakers. They took us to the Khabarovsk Sports Palace, where at a Japanese exhibition of consumer goods, just closed, more than fifty Japanese firms displayed some seventeen thousand items. Seventy-five thousand Russians visited the twelve-day show. At the Khabarovsk City Museum a display of Japanese art was in progress. Excavations for a new tourist hotel were under way adjacent to the Sports Palace on the Amur River embankment. It was to be a thirteen-story building, the largest in the city, primarily for visitors from Japan. A new Intourist hotel was being built in Irkutsk for the same purpose.

The farther I went in eastern Siberia, the more I heard and saw of the Japanese. They dominated the travel routes and they dominated the great new port of Nakhodka which the Russians had built since World War II on a peninsula south of Vladivostok. It was a beautiful site, landlocked like San Francisco, with fine hills coming down to form connected lagoons, and miles and miles of safe anchorage. In this basin, warmed by the Japan current and ice-free the year round (unlike Vladivostok), the Russians had constructed a modern mechanized port. There were scores of piers, all with rail trackage, moving cranes and derricks, floating docks and repair yards. In the port lay freighters of all nationalities, but more Japanese than any other kind but Soviet. Some four hundred Japanese freighters had visited Nakhodka in 1965, even more in 1966.

As the Trans-Siberian rolled through the broad valley of the Ussuri toward the Pacific, I was struck by the richness of the land, the green meadows, the fine forested hills, the soft temperate climate—and the scantiness of habitation. There were few evidences of large-scale agriculture, only tiny private gardens hacked out beside peasant cottages. What could easily be Russia's California looked like a raw frontier. I remembered the surprise of a Russian whom I once met in San Francisco. "This is nothing like Vladivostok," he said. "I am a little disappointed. I expected to see Indians and log cabins. But San Francisco is another New York."

"We are so far from Moscow," the residents of the Maritimes said. "We lack people and means to develop the land."

That this was true I had no doubt. In the Soviet five-year plans the Far East and the Maritime Province got low priority. The distance from European industry, the high cost of transportation, the sparseness of population, the competition for available funds— all these tended to hold back the pace of development.

But now, as I was told in Tokyo, the Russians had proposed an answer to the dilemma of Far Eastern development. The name of the answer was Japan. They had drafted elaborate schemes which would cost many billions of dollars and had invited the Japanese to participate—at a profit. In effect, they were offering the Japanese an economic partnership on a basis such as the Soviet Union had not proposed to foreign business since Lenin during the period of NEP (the New Economic Policy) asked the foreign concessionaires to return to Russia to help put the sagging Bolshevik economy on its feet back in the early 1920's.

The Soviet proposals had been advanced at a joint meeting of Soviet and Japanese businessmen in Tokyo by Mikhail V. Nesterov, chairman of the Soviet Chamber of Commerce. He called for Japanese capital investments on an open-ended basis. They would be repaid under an arrangement whereby Japan would receive a substantial share of the production of the newly created industries— large chemical, fertilizer, cement, metallurgical, petroleum, natural gas, harbor, rail, pipeline and mining enterprises.

The first project was to be a gas pipeline from newly discovered gas fields in Sakhalin. The line would bring the gas to ports for transfer to special compressor ships and delivery both to Japan and Siberia. The scheme had attracted immediate Japanese interest because of their shortage of fuel and gas, particularly in Hokkaido and northern Honshu. The Japanese would provide the technical facilities, build the pipeline and receive in return natural gas.

A similar project had been outlined for an oil pipeline in eastern Siberia which would supply the growing Soviet industrial centers there as well as providing oil for the Japanese tankers.

As sketched by the Russians, the needs of Siberian development (in which they encompassed most of the region east of the Urals) were too vast to be met by Japanese production alone. They estimated that Siberia would require 24 to 29 million tons of oil by 1970 and 66 to 76 million tons by 1975. To keep pace with this demand, the Russians were projecting the construction of 7,760 kilometers of pipeline in Siberia. They suggested that they contract the delivery to Japan of 10 to 20 million tons of oil per year, beginning in 1970, in return for assistance in building the pipelines— a $2 billion project.

Pointing out that they had timber reserves of 4,200 million cubic yards in the Far Eastern region, the Russians suggested that Japan provide timber mills and wood-processing equipment in return for export of finished and unfinished lumber.

The Russians acknowledged that development of Siberia on such a scale would tax even the expanded capacity of Nakhodka and Vladivostok (which they indicated soon would be reopened to general ship traffic). They proposed that the Japanese assist them in building another new port with large and modern facilities capable of handling freighters up to twenty thousand tons.

The Japanese readily confessed to me that the Soviet proposals had fallen on receptive ears. Already Japan's trade with Russia had topped the $400 million mark, and the Japanese, looking for new and profitable markets for venture capital and their rapidly expanding technical resources, found the notion of a Siberian partnership attractive. Their only fear was that Russia's capital needs might go beyond their own resources. They also wanted to recapture their investment more rapidly than the twenty-year repayment period proposed by Moscow.

There was another factor involved, I was told. The Russians made no secret that their advances to the Japanese bore a direct connection to the Sino-Soviet split. The Russians were not suggesting that Japan align herself with the Soviet Union against China. But everyone knew that the *rapprochement* between Moscow and Tokyo closely paralleled the growing hostility between Moscow and Peking. Trade between the two countries had not resumed until 1958, just before the Sino-Soviet rift began to come into the open. Before that relations had been plagued by the aftermath of World War II, the lack of a formal peace treaty and the Soviet occupation of four Kuriles Islands which Japan hoped to regain.

The Japanese never stopped reminding the Russians of their desire for return of the islands. They had been put off again and again, but they suspected that at some appropriate moment Moscow would announce that she was returning at least two islands—a satisfactory compromise. What had held up the return thus far, the Japanese believed, was Russia's fear of setting a precedent. Japan was not the only country which had territorial claims against the Soviet Union. Rumania, for instance, bore a grudge because of Soviet absorption of Bessarabia. There was the complicated and potentially explosive question of the exchange of lands whereby Poland had been compensated for Soviet accessions in eastern Poland and the western Ukraine with equivalent German territories.

Most serious of all were the Chinese territorial claims. The total area involved was enormous. According to Chinese calculation, the Soviet Union had taken over 3,886,000 square kilometers of Chinese or Chinese-dominated territory—5,326,000 if Outer Mongolia was included. These areas had a resident population of more than thirty million.

The Chinese had made a point of linking their territorial claims with those of other nations, specifically urging the Japanese and the Rumanians to press their demands.

In such a situation, the Japanese recognized, Moscow was bound to exercise caution in satisfying one request lest it establish a precedent for another.

Beyond these matters loomed others. Japan, I was told, felt a "special relationship" toward China. This was a product of their common heritage. Japan, after all, was a younger sister of China —historically, culturally. Her language, her traditions, her philosophy had been derived from China. The two nations were entwined by thousands of years of contact and conflict. And there was a deeper, more intimate, personal and psychological bond which stemmed from the long war and Japanese occupation of the 1920's, the 1930's and the 1940's.

Two or three generations of Japanese had, in one way or another, dedicated their lives to China. They had served in armies of occupation. They had fought the Chinese and ruled great portions of China. Japanese industrialists habitually thought of China as Japan's natural economic partner. The coal and steel of Manchuria, which they so long controlled, seemed to them a natural complement to Japan's consumer and light industry orientation.

More than any other people, the Japanese felt that they *knew* China. They felt a sense of obligation to China, a duty that they must fulfill. This was particularly true of Japanese Army men and occupation officials, some of whom had spent half their adult lives in Manchuria. In this feeling there was often a mixture of both guilt and nostalgia—guilt for the crimes which Japan had inflicted upon China and nostalgia for the country itself, its people and its way of life. Japan was filled with "old China hands."

"We Japanese understand China," an older army man told me. "We have lived there. We know what they are thinking and what they really mean. It is very difficult for a Westerner or one who does not know China to understand her."

Again and again I heard Japanese refer to Japan's "special role" with respect to China. They defined this "special role" as that of mediator between the aroused ideologies of Peking and the strident military spokesmen in Washington. They saw themselves as interpreters of the West to China and of China to the West.

For the most part, Japan's Sinophiles were not leftists, not ideological supporters of the Peking regime. To the contrary, they were solid conservatives, even reactionaries. They were retired generals with shaven heads and graven faces, hardened in a thousand battles. They were the tough senior members of the big family business combines. They were former diplomats, politicians of the generation before World War II, right-wing members of the Diet. They were men who were Japanese first, Asians second. Men who envisaged Japan as an Asian and a Pacific power. Men who accepted Japan's orientation toward the West and the United States as a necessary, even inevitable, consequence of defeat in war, but who still thought in terms of the Japanese dream of an "East Asia Co-prosperity Sphere." Men who saw in the rise of a modern, nationalist, industrialized China a profound force. They told me they looked toward a partnership with that force. If they verbalized their feelings (which for the most part they did not), they suggested that Japan could give leadership to the inchoate strength of China. Japan had the experience. She knew the West. She knew banking, commerce, finance, international trade, international relations. She knew modern warfare. These Japanese saw themselves as providing nascent China with the direction, the inclination and the know-how which would enable the partnership (although this they hardly dared think even in private) to achieve the aims which had been lost in World War II. Japan, they knew, could no longer think of conquering China and using that continent-country as a base for world conquest. But hand in hand with China, what could not such a formidable combination achieve?

It was men who dreamed such dreams who went to Peking again and again, who composed the friendship groups and quasi-government delegations which were entertained in China and, in their turn, entertained the Chinese in Japan. They visited China in large numbers.

More Japanese visited China than any other nationals—4,400 in 1965 and upwards of 5,000 in 1966. Only four hundred Chinese paid return calls. There were more Japanese newsmen in China— nine—than represented any other country. There were nine Chinese newsmen in Tokyo. The Japanese press consistently published more news of China, more firsthand reports, more information gleaned from visitors, more data from official Chinese reports than appeared anywhere else.

Despite this intercourse the two countries did not have formal diplomatic relations. The demand of China sympathizers in Japan for establishment of diplomatic ties ebbed and flowed. The Chinese did not press the point.

Just as Japan's trade with Russia began to grow with the cooling of Sino-Soviet relations, so did Japan's trade with China. In 1965 Japan emerged as China's principal trading partner, replacing Hong Kong (earlier it had been the Soviet Union) as the chief source of Chinese sales and purchases. The volume of China-Japan trade in 1966 crossed the half-billion-dollar mark, double what it was as recently as 1964. China, of course, was compelled to turn to capitalist countries when the Soviet Union and the Communist bloc applied their economic sanctions. In 1965 the Japanese sold China $70 million in fertilizers, $45 million in machinery and $45 million in steel products. Japan bought from China $45 million in soya products, $26 million in rice and $24 million in pig iron.

Japan's trade increased so rapidly with China that the Japanese became somewhat embarrassed, particularly when American eyebrows began to rise. They hurried to point out that their trade had not grown more than that of some West European countries. West Germany, for instance, expanded its China trade 97 percent, Italy 129 percent and Great Britain 29 percent.

But could Japan continue indefinitely to trade on a massive scale, with both China and Russia? I did not think so and my doubt was shared by many Japanese businessmen and diplomats. If compelled to choose, which partner did Japan prefer?

Emotionally, the Japanese preferred China as a partner. They had no empathy for Russia. Japan launched its career as a great power by defeating Russia in 1905. The Japanese had aspired to take over all the Maritimes and Siberia as far west as Baikal in the period of intervention and civil war (and probably would have succeeded had it not been for a stubborn and punctilious American expeditionary general named Graves). They had learned to respect Soviet military strength in two undeclared wars in the 1930's. The savage attack launched by the special Soviet Far Eastern armies in the closing days of World War II had confirmed Japanese estimates of the striking power of the Red Army. Nothing which had happened in the post-Stalin and post-Khrushchev years had really modified the basic Japanese hostility toward and fear of Communist Russia.

Compelled to choose between Russia and China, I thought Japan's instincts would incline her toward China. And yet it was more complex than that.

There was the question, for example, of the atom bomb.

It had been twenty-one years since Hiroshima. I arrived in Japan only a few days before the anniversary. I found no lack of talk about the bomb, about Hiroshima, about Japan's attitude. Particularly in the ancient capital of Kyoto Japanese thoughts turned to the bomb. Kyoto had been spared, and on the anniversary of Hiroshima's tragedy Kyoto pondered the event and its implications. Thus it had been each year since 1945. But this year there was a great difference. This was made plain by the August issues of the great Japanese magazines, the popular picture magazines, the Japanese equivalents of *Life* and *Look*, the serious magazines, those which play the role of *Harper's* and the *Atlantic*.

A friend of mine picked up a copy of a Japanese picture magazine and showed it to me. "Take a look at this," he said. "Here is real news." I looked at the magazine. I could see nothing unusual about it.

"For the first time since 1945," my friend said, "they have not devoted the whole issue to Hiroshima. And this is not the only magazine. Look over the newsstand and you will find that none devotes its August issue exclusively to Hiroshima. Never since 1945 has this happened. Japan is changing."

Indeed, she was. It was not only the magazines. Not only the memorial meetings, the great annual rally and outpouring of Japanese pacifism, the huge assemblies devoted to the crusade against the bomb. The gatherings were smaller than any that had been held since the war, and the reason was not merely the controversy which had broken out between Japanese authorities and the radically split delegations of the peace movement, the hard-liners representing Peking and its Afro-Asian group, and the disciplined group representing the Soviet Union.

The plain fact was that the mystique which had made Hiroshima a magic word and a movement to stir the spirits of men had begun to fade.

I felt it was not merely the passage of time which had accomplished this. It was the change in Japanese dynamics, the slow emergence of Japan from the trauma of the war. For years after 1945 Japan had turned in upon herself, like a patient who has undergone major surgery and survived by a hairsbreadth. Japan in this period was willing—even eager—to let the United States make the hard decisions, to let American military power protect her, to depend upon the warm reassurance of American aid and American trade, to turn her back on the Asia which had been the scene of her great national tragedy, to abjure any real role in international affairs, to ignore Russia and forget China, to let dreams of Southeast Asia and of empire fade from consciousness. These were the years of Japan's idealistic embracement of pacifism, her stand against an army, against military power, against the atom bomb and nuclear warfare. For years nothing penetrated the cocoon within which Japan wrapped herself. When Russia announced in 1949 that she now possessed the atom bomb, Japan did not quiver. The only reaction in Tokyo was deep regret that this dangerous, antihuman weapon had now passed into other hands. For herself she felt safe and comfortable under the protection of American nuclear power.

But now times were changing. The war lay a good twenty years back. The physical restoration of Japan had long since been completed. More than completed—Japan had emerged as one of the world's great industrial powers. With only one-seventh China's population, Japan's production was above that of China. She was already No. 3 in the world in steel and electric power capacity. By 1970 she would be second only to the United States and the Soviet Union in total economic capability.

Slowly the Japanese were beginning to perceive this fact and slowly they were beginning to think about its consequences.

"For years," a man who had lived in Japan half a lifetime told me, "Japan suffered from an inferiority complex. This goes back to her nineteenth-century effort to emulate the West. Now, for the first time, some Japanese are beginning to see that they no longer need feel inferior to the West. They have caught up in industry, in technology, in standard of living. And some are beginning to add up what this means in terms of world power."

What it meant was that Japan had the economic and industrial power, she had the finance capital and the technological know-how to play an imposing role on the world scene. She was prepared technically to give Asia leadership in the struggle of the backward continent to achieve the efficiency and comfort of the machine age. But she lacked several essentials.

Could Japan take the leadership of Asia without a military establishment and without nuclear arms? Could she become the world's No. 3 power without atom bombs if other, weaker nations possessed them?

This was the question which was forcefully impinging upon the thinking of the Japanese. The question was on the agenda before China exploded her first nuclear device. It was beginning to be talked about when China exploded her second device. When the third Chinese explosion occurred in 1966, its impact resounded more loudly in Japan than in any other nation.

No talk had been heard in Japan about nuclear arms when Russia exploded her first bomb. None was heard when the China sequence started. But bomb No. 3 and bomb No. 4 broke it.

"China frightens them," an American diplomat told me. "Russia didn't. They felt that the umbrella of U.S. power protected them. But there is something different in their reaction to China, especially the new tests. Now they see China well on the way to nuclear armament. This has shaken them."

What would be the result?

As in India, the Japanese political leaders would not speak to me frankly for quotation. They clung to the safe, familiar clichés.

But in private they spoke differently. They admitted that China's bomb had changed the whole question.

"How can we ignore it?" one said. "The world is changing. China has changed. We must, too."

"Don't think we haven't counted the cost," said an adviser to the government. "We know that it would mean an unlimited world nuclear arms race. But what is the alternative? If Geneva fails; if India, for instance, should start to build the bomb, we could not stay out."

Of all the nonnuclear powers Japan had the fewest barriers to cross. She possessed an industry and a technology, a corps of scientists and physicists superior to those of at least two nuclear powers (France and China) and at least equal to those of another (Britain). Some Japanese felt they could match paces with any nuclear power except the United States. To be sure, most of Japan's nuclear physicists opposed the bomb on principle. They were dedicated pacifists. But the technology and industry of nuclear armament were now so well known that this did not impose much impediment.

Japan possessed another advantage when, as and if she entered the nuclear arms race. She alone among nonnuclear powers was far advanced toward development of a delivery system. Here again she stood next to the United States and the Soviet Union. While deliberately holding back in nuclear development, Japan had embarked on a vigorous program of space exploration. She was well along toward production of satellite launchers and the hardware equally useful for sending a Telstar or a Sputnik into orbit or lobbing a missile across the Pacific.

Japanese development of nuclear power for generating electricity and for ship propulsion would enable her scientists easily to shift to weapons work. The satellite program would provide the know-how for missiles.

"We thought we could hold back popular sentiment for nuclear arms by getting ahead in the space race," a Japanese military analyst said. "It may not work out exactly as some of us expected."

I was fascinated to know why Japan had been so moved by China's development of nuclear weapons. It seemed clear that her reaction must be mixed up with the strange skein of emotions which bound Japan to China in a kind of love-hate complex.

Could it also be that the Japanese really feared China?

I asked Edwin O. Reischauer, who had just come back to Tokyo from Washington to announce his resignation as U.S. Ambassador. He felt that the Japanese did not fear China, that they felt a confidence in their ability to cope with China. They would not rush blindly toward nuclear arms just because China possessed them.

But other diplomats disagreed. They thought that the Japanese did fear China, even though not admitting it. They felt the Japanese feared China's size, the sheer mass of her population, the rapid expansion of her industrial capabilities, her obvious military power and the increasing aggressiveness with which she expressed herself in international affairs.

"Two things have shaken the Japanese," an American diplomat said. "First, the latest Chinese nuclear test. This really hit home. And now the crisis in Peking. It has been so savage and so many of the individuals are those well known here in Japan."

A Japanese said: "Perhaps we are not afraid of China, but she has made us stop and think."

It semed to me that this Japanese put the question in the most realistic perspective. The Japanese had convinced themselves that they knew China, understood her, could manage her, could handle Chinese problems which no one else could tackle.

Now they were beginning to lose this confidence. Businessmen were returning from Peking bewildered. They found it impossible to talk to Chinese officials with whom they had been dealing for several years.

"They are rushing from meeting to meeting," a Japanese said. "They are spending so much time absorbing the 'thought of Chairman Mao' that they have no time to talk trade or sign contracts. Literally, they seem to have only about an hour a day to put in at their desks."

Japanese newspapermen in Peking reported the same thing. They reported even more. They told of the savage antiforeignism of the Red Guards. They described the danger to a foreigner of even appearing on the streets of Peking, of the precautions which the Chinese Foreign Office urged all diplomats to take to avoid incidents. The names which came up in the Chinese press as targets of attack, the institutions which the Red Guards assaulted—these were precisely those with which the Japanese felt a common bond. Many of the sacked officials had been to Tokyo or had entertained the Japanese in China. The writers who were excoriated were men known in Japan. Their writings had been translated and published in Tokyo. The works of art which the young Chinese took from the museums and shipped to the warehouses were treasures of China's national culture, known to and venerated by the Japanese. The rising winds of Chinese xenophobia and chauvinism began to alarm even the most Sinophile of the Japanese. For the first time they began to stand back and ask: "Do we really *know* China?"

It was a question worth asking and difficult to answer. But the implications seemed to me more than disquieting. If Japan did not understand China, who did? If Japan could not act as a bridge between China and the world, who could? If China was turning her back not only on everything European and Western but upon Europeanized Asia as well, then where could common ground be found?

Did the new turn in China mean that all Japan's nostalgic dreams about China would go up in smoke? There seemed a good possibility of this. Small wonder, then, that the Japanese began to talk with seriousness for the first time since August 8, 1945, of rearmament—of nuclear armament, of possessing the weapons which were needed if she were to take a seat at the table of world power reserved for those who backed their play with fission or fusion.

The view I had had of China from many Asian countries had

been a formidable one. Often it held elements of mystery. Sometimes there were forebodings of danger. But, it seemed to me, the view from Tokyo was the most enigmatic of all and potentially the most frightening. Perhaps the Japanese had deceived themselves about the depth of their understanding of China. Perhaps they had lost the thread during the quarter-century or more in which they had been overlords in China, or in the nearly twenty years since Communism came to the top. Perhaps Oriental background, common history, shared philosophy, mutual culture and art were not as useful keys to interpretation as Japan thought.

Yet, if this were true, where then did one turn for knowledge? From what source was interpretation to be drawn? I had traveled the Lo Wu Road and had found it ending in a tiny village which was, for practical purposes, a cul-de-sac. Here were the Japanese. They had traveled every road which existed that led to China. What had it profited them?

I spent a day or two in Kyoto, Japan's ancient capital. I had found it difficult to get a grasp of Japan or of Japanness in the neon-lighted Americanized traffic arteries of Tokyo. In Kyoto the sense of Japan's timelessness came to me from the ancient gardens, the three-hundred-year-old inn, the gentle and graceful customs of the teahouse and the temple. Here was a permanence, a continuity which had survived a revolution more violent than any which was now sweeping China. For Japan had been through the revolution of the industrial process. She had seen the machine sweep her feudalism into the dustbin. Japan had endured the conquests of her militarists, the terror of her fascists and the bitterest of all torments—defeat and disaster in the world's first nuclear war. Only she had endured this. Only she knew its cataclysmic and revolutionary effects. Beside these experiences, it seemed to me, even the reformation and destruction of China's ways which were going on under Communism and which were being given so spectacular a tempo by Mao's Red Guards were relatively superficial. Could it not be that within the vastness of China there persisted the elements of the same Chinaness which I now breathed in the elemental quiet and purity of a temple garden? Only time would tell. But time, I had now learned, was told on another clock in Asia. I did not think that Mao could yet contend that he had changed all the clocks of China.

12
The Secret Cities

I FIRST BEGAN TO HEAR TALK OF CHINA AND THE ATOM BOMB IN 1959 and 1960 from the Russians. At diplomatic receptions or dinners a Soviet diplomat or correspondent or, sometimes, a general would get into conversation with me and the talk would drift to the subject of nuclear arms and the danger to the world of a nuclear arms race.

"The United States and Russia must come to an agreement," the Russian would say. "We have got to get an agreement on nuclear arms and disarmament before *they* get the weapon. Otherwise it will be *very* difficult and *very* dangerous."

"They" in this context was China.

I had such conversations with a number of Soviet officials over several years. So many times and so often did it follow precisely the same pattern that it could be no accident. It clearly represented a prevailing Soviet point of view.

It was equally clear what lay behind it. The Chinese had expressed themselves on the question of nuclear warfare. Mao Tsetung himself had spoken at the 1957 conference of Communist leaders in Moscow. He had said, in effect, that nuclear warfare would be a catastrophe for the world. It might destroy half the world's population. Even more. But those who survived would be Communists. And from the ruins and ashes of the world a new civilization would rise, the most beautiful that had ever been seen, a Communist civilization. As for China herself, should she become engaged in nuclear war, she would lose possibly 300 million people. But, added Mao, 300 million would survive.

The Russians did not think this attitude toward nuclear warfare boded well for the world or for China's conduct when, as and if she got the bomb. The Russians for their part wanted no war which left half the world destroyed. As for Mao's blithe comment that though 300 million Chinese would die in a nuclear war 300 million would survive, the Russians shook their heads. No other country in the world could make remarks like that. No other country possessed such a population.

When Mao began to talk of the United States as a "paper tiger," Khrushchev reminded him that this "paper tiger" had "nuclear teeth." There was no doubt that Khrushchev was speaking for his countrymen when he sought vainly to convince the Chinese that nuclear war was no joke.

At that time the Chinese did not have a nuclear capability and the question was temporarily academic. Indeed, the usual forecasts appeared in the West that there was no need to worry because the Chinese could never build the bomb. They didn't have the industry, the scientists or the know-how. Wasn't it well known what a mess they had made of their backyard steel furnaces? A country which could not even make its own automobiles could hardly be taken seriously as a potential nuclear power. As for the Russian warnings— just a Soviet trick to try to get us to agree to a nuclear deal which might undercut our freedom of action.

To me this seemed a totally familiar line of reasoning. It was almost identical with that which I had heard advanced concerning the Soviet Union between 1945 and 1949. Then, too, there was a great school of scoffers who insisted that the Soviet could never build the bomb, or at best that it would take twenty to twenty-five years. The number of specialists who predicted a Soviet bomb four years after Hiroshima could be counted on the fingers of one hand— with some fingers left over.

One of the objectives of my long journey around China's periphery was to get an accurate assessment of her military potential, particularly her nuclear capability, present and future. I could think of nothing more fatuous—and dangerous—than to underestimate the striking power of a nation which many Americans regarded as their most deadly enemy.

There were two aspects to this question: How strong was China and how did she intend to employ that strength? Until we could assess accurately the weight of Chinese power, we could hardly determine the seriousness of her intentions.

I put my question to specialists in every country I visited. I cross-examined the diplomats and the men and women who had traveled to and from China. I found a wide range of opinions concerning China's military potential, largely depending upon estimates of her rate of economic growth. But there were other factors, too—chiefly prejudice and wishful thinking.

For example, a brilliant Thai statesman, a man who had a generally realistic grasp on Asian affairs, seriously insisted to me that China would not be ready to put the world to serious challenge for at least fifty years. His estimate, however, was based on his fierce antagonism to China, his hatred for Communism, his complete unwillingness to accept the reality of Chinese achievements. He scoffed at the Chinese nuclear tests and shrugged his shoulders at the People's Liberation Army.

This view was not shared by any military man with whom I spoke, including some of the Thai commanders. An extremely well-informed Japanese intelligence expert estimated that China would be ready to challenge the world powers within ten years—if her present pace of development was maintained. A Russian official dourly insisted that China had already begun her challenge.

The truth, it seemed to me, lay somewhere in between.

The most serious and careful analysis of China's nuclear capability which I was able to obtain was that of an American specialist who had access to most—if not all—of the key intelligence data. He advanced the hypothesis that China was engaged in what amounted to a nuclear "Great Leap Forward." She was moving directly into the hydrogen bomb phase, in his opinion, completely by-passing the conventional atomic or fission weapon.

The same specialist suggested that China had decided not to build strategic bombers but to leap directly to the missile delivery of nuclear warheads.

The principal support for this hypothesis came from the three China nuclear tests which had been carried out by mid-1966. The last test was of a fission device wrapped in an enriched uranium blanket. This was not a full fusion package, but it showed that China had the technology to create a hydrogen bomb and that her next test could well be of a hydrogen bomb.

This specialist said bluntly: "The worst error we could make is to underestimate China. Based on the data we have, she may already *have* the H-bomb."

He held the view that China was substantially further advanced toward nuclear capability than most Western estimates had supposed. A specialist in Japan supported this opinion. He calculated that China's Spring 1966 nuclear test showed a development rate at least two or three years ahead of the capability forecasts made by the chief Western analysts as recently as 1965.

There was no agreement among the intelligence community as to when China would possess both hydrogen warheads and intercontinental ballistics with which to deliver them.

"She may well surprise us all," the American expert said. "Most of us are guessing it will take ten years. They have Russian surface-to-surface missiles which they acquired before 1958. We know that development is going ahead rapidly, probably using the Soviet missiles as prototypes."

Another specialist suggested it would take China ten years to perfect a system which would enable her to lay down missiles on the continental United States or upon targets in European Russia.

"But she will have medium missiles before that," he added. "They are testing ballistics missiles right now, and, of course, those tests are being monitored—probably by both the United States and the Soviet Union."

A suggestion that China would require a decade to perfect long-range missiles brought little reassurance to countries in Asia, like India and Japan. Both nations lay within easy range of conventional bombers, which could be converted for the delivery of A-bombs if the Chinese wished. The Chinese could also attack Mongolia or Siberia, although these actions would subject her to the risk of nuclear retaliation by the United States, the Soviet Union or both.

Secretary of Defense Robert McNamara estimated in an address in Paris before the NATO powers in December, 1965, that China might have intermediate missile capability by 1967 and intercontinental capability by 1975. In Europe and America it was thought that he was exaggerating. Asians thought that he was understating the case. Japanese intelligence spokesmen said the Chinese already had missiles of 450-to-650-mile range. They first began to test them in 1963. They believed that the Chinese now had a satellite launcher with a 1,200-mile capability—just a step or two from intercontinental range. Another intelligence official told me the Chinese had already tested missiles with ranges of more than 2 thousand miles.

The remarkable accuracy of the Japanese intelligence estimate was confirmed almost as soon as I returned to the United States. The Chinese fourth nuclear test—the firing in October, 1966, of a meduim-range missile with a nuclear warhead—stunned many Americans and not a few Asians. But it perfectly fitted the intelli-- gence data which had been publicly available.

The shock which emanated from the fourth China test resulted from the consistent downgrading of Chinese potentials by ill-informed or deliberately tendentious military sources. The firing demonstrated to all of China's Asian neighbors that they were now within range of Chinese nuclear weapons. It demonstrated that only a few years—a very few years—separated China from a transoceanic nuclear capability.

Where did China's nuclear development stem from?

In the first place, the Chinese had a cadre of brilliant physicists. They had been trained at Cambridge, at Columbia, at the Massachusetts and California Institutes of Technology, at Russia's Dubna Institute. They had the technical and scientific background which they needed to move forward to the creation of nuclear weaponry. They had hoped and expected to get from the Soviet Union not only technical and scientific expertise but completed weapons, delivery systems and plants for the construction of nuclear arms. However, with the break between Moscow and Peking this went down the drain. In fact, Soviet reluctance to provide the Chinese with nuclear hardware and nuclear production facilities played a major role in the break. It was a blow to China, but by no means a fatal one.

The Chinese had gone forward on their own, basing themselves on two "secret cities," each located at the farthest remove from coastal areas or possible means of attack.

The first of the cities to be developed was Lanchow in China's northwest province of Kansu. It was picked because it had an excellent power source, and uranium conversion required immense amounts of electric power. Some indication of the effort which China pumped into nuclear development could be gained from the fact that Lanchow boomed from a population of under 400,000 in 1953 to an estimated three million at the time of the "Great Leap Forward" in 1959. It dropped back sharply in the "rectification" which occurred in the following years and now was estimated at between one and one and a half million.

Great power installations had been built on the Hwang Ho River, and the region now produced about 1 percent of China's total of forty billion kilowatt-hours of electricity. It was estimated that if only 35 percent of Lanchow's power was used for nuclear purposes, it could turn out 1,700 pounds of uranium a year, enough for fifty bombs.

It was typical of the tendency of the intelligence community to underestimate China that in 1963 U.S. experts calculated that the Lanchow gaseous diffusion plant would not be able to turn out enriched uranium before 1968 or 1969. In fact, the Chinese beat the estimates by nearly five years.

Lanchow was not only China's leading nuclear center. It was also a rapidly growing petrochemical region with a two-million-ton oil refinery to serve the Yümen oil fields, the largest in China.

For years the West had known little about Lanchow except what could be derived from U-2 overflights, satellite recordings and scientific espionage. Now, however, the industrial capability of the city had grown to the point that the Chinese had begun to bring in foreign experts. Their movements and activities were carefully circumscribed. Security was intense. Yet it was not possible to keep everything under wraps. There were more than a hundred foreign specialists working in Lanchow in 1966. Some were West German engineers installing a petrochemical plant. Some were British and Dutch, helping to erect fertilizer and synthetic-fiber factories.

The second nuclear center was Paotow. As recently as 1949 Paotow had been a pleasant back-country cattle-trading town. It had a population of forty thousand and was of interest to no one but travelers in Inner Mongolia. Its streets were unpaved. There was no industry.

Today it was the site of two plutonium reactors. It had acquired a steel mill with a capacity of two to three million tons, started by the Russians before they pulled out their experts, and still unfinished because only one of four projected blast furnaces had been completed by the Chinese. Its population had risen to 500,000.

The small Paotow reactors produced only enough fissionable material to make two or three bombs a year. However, with the availability of Lanchow's enriched uranium their output was pushed far higher.

The range which the Chinese employed for testing their bombs and missiles was located near Lake Lob Nor in Sinkiang province.

While these were the principal Chinese nuclear facilities, the ones whose existence was public knowledge in the West, the specialists with whom I talked did not feel that this exhausted

China's nuclear resources. There were others. Some possibly had not been detected. Some were known to be in the construction stage. Chinese technical and scientific capacity was rapidly expanding. There seemed little limit to its ultimate scope except factors arising within China itself. As the Red Guard movement increased in momentum, sweeping out of its way all vestiges of Westernism, including Western thought, scientific theory and even threatening the fundamentals of education, there appeared the possibility that a kind of Chinese Know-Nothingism might arise which would temporarily hinder China's scientific progress and her ability to expand her nuclear capability.

The fact that she had been able to move so rapidly seemed to stem from her ability to concentrate available resources. It reminded me of the Soviet Union. Even some of the terminology was the same. The Chinese had set up eight special "Ministries of Machine-Building" to carry forward military technology. In Russia when the late Police Chief Lavrenti P. Beriya was charged with responsibility for putting Russia into the atomic league, his special apparatus was called "the Ministry of Medium Machine-Building." The title was retained even after Beriya was liquidated and long after the nuclear effort was taken out of the hands of the Soviet secret police.

The Chinese had never announced the purposes of the eight Ministries of Machine-Building. But from the biographies of the officials connected with them deductions could be drawn. Ministry No. 1, for instance, certainly concerned heavy industry; Ministry No. 2, nuclear engineering; No. 3, arms development; No. 4, communications and electronics devices; No. 5, missiles; No. 6, naval devices; No. 7, aeronautics; No. 8, agricultural machinery and tanks.

The Chinese had concentrated possibly 5 percent of their top scientists in these endeavors. The concentration went far to equalize the over-all poverty of Chinese resources.

But, by any terms of analysis, nuclear weaponry was still the Chinese arm of the future. What gave China power today was her conventional forces. No military man whom I met on the periphery of China had any tendency to underestimate the People's Liberation Army. In the thin and foggy elevations of the Himalayas, along the stormy course of the Black Dragon River in Siberia or in Cambodia's steaming jungle the word was the same: The People's Liberation Army, man for man, was the best fighting force in Asia, possibly the world.

Lin Piao once characterized the Chinese Army as the equal of any in the world—up to the distance of two hundred meters. Or within rifle range. A Japanese military man who had served in China for many years agreed with this estimate. "Within China's frontiers," he said, "her army is very, very strong."

The emphasis on the army's skill within a range of two hundred meters had a very specific meaning. The PLA was being trained to fight and kill at the closest possible range. It was trained to fight hand to hand in close combat, employing the bayonet, the dagger or the knife. By fighting at such close range, the PLA generals pointed out, they could neutralize the modern weapons of the enemy. Planes, artillery, rockets—none of these were of value to soldiers fighting man to man or within grenade-tossing distance.

The Liberation Army was born in the Chinese Communist Party's long struggle for power. It was an instrument created by Mao Tse-tung, specifically for that struggle. It was tempered in years of the most difficult fighting against the longest of odds.

The days of the Long March were thirty years in the past. But the essential toughness and strength of the army still harked back to Yenan. Today the army comprised a force of between 2.5 and 2.6 million men, making up 107 infantry divisions of the triangular type, 26 artillery divisions, 4 armored divisions, 3 cavalry and 3 airborne divisions. In addition, there were 15 divisions of border troops and a militia which ran between 7 and 12 millions, depending on how you made up your estimate. A one-year increase in the conscript tour of service was lifting the PLA total by 500,000 to 800,000 men.

Whoever I asked—American, Indian, Japanese, English—rated the

PLA a fine fighting force, high in morale, well officered, well trained, disciplined. It was good in mountain and jungle fighting. It was good at night maneuvers. It was accustomed to operating without much in the way of transport or communications. It could live off the land and fight with nothing but rifles, ammunition, a little artillery and no air support. Its tactics had been refined in the Korean War. Its equipment was rough and ready by Western or even Russian standards. Most Chinese artillery dated back to World War II or earlier. It had little radar, little signal equipment. The air force was primitive.

For transportation the PLA still relied on its own feet. Chinese vehicle production was low. The country turned out fewer than twenty thousand trucks and cars a year and not more than twenty thousand tractors. The PLA did not have the mobility of gasoline transport.

"This might make some difference in the south," a specialist said. "When the Chinese went into Korea, they had the benefit of Soviet logistics. And they were close to their own bases in Manchuria. But the basic motive power of the PLA is still the human being. That's the way they are set up. In some situations it is a weakness. But in jungles or in the mountains or the wilderness it is a strength.

"The PLA is trained to fight and to hike. And to hike and to fight. There are worse ways of conditioning a combat force."

Despite the alarms and excursions of 1966, the PLA continued to be disposed in much the same way as it had been since the end of the Korean War. That is, 95 percent of the troops were located east of Tibet and east of Sinkiang. The big concentrations were still in the area of Peking and of Manchuria, readily available for any threat which might come from Korea or Siberia. The second large grouping was opposite Taiwan. There was no major concentration to the south in the region adjacent to Vietnam.

There had been some redisposition of the Chinese Air Force. A number of squadrons were shifted to the south in preparation to meet possible air strikes from Southeast Asia. However, the air arm was one of China's weakest links. They had no more than 2,500 planes, largely Soviet or Soviet prototypes. They built their own MIG-19's with facilities provided by Russia before the break. They had a handful of MIG-21's and no production capability. Their antiaircraft system was not strong, although they had some SAM-2 missiles which they got before the break with Moscow. However, as late as 1963 they had only eight SAM sites.

The Chinese Navy was even less of a force than the air arm. The Chinese were estimated to dispose fewer than 50 destroyers and escorts, mostly coastal craft, 150 motor torpedo boats and 100 other naval craft. They could not land more than 75,000 lightly armed troops. They had a few submarines, which the Russians gave them, and were starting to build their own in Port Arthur. Some Japanese experts thought these might be nuclear-armed submarines. This seemed unlikely to me. It did not fit the over-all picture of Chinese industrial capability.

Her industrial establishment was considerably better than the cartoon-like image left by the ill-fated experiment in "backyard steel mills." Actually, her steel production in 1966 ran close to 12 million tons compared with U.S. figures of close to 125 million and Soviet totals of over 100. But 12 million tons can be made to go a long way in a primitive country which does not use steel for consumer purposes; which does not possess a steel-devouring automotive industry; which does not use steel in houses or buildings, in large-scale highway construction or in the thousand and one means by which Western Europe and America employ steel. Russia managed to stay on in the war and press Nazi Germany to defeat with a steel production of less than 12 million tons. China had a total electric power production of only 40 billion kilowatts. But the Soviet Union had no more in 1949 when they turned out their first A-bomb. China's chemical fertilizer production was 4.5 million tons in 1965. That was more than Russia made in 1955. China had a cement production of 8 to 10 million tons, a crude oil output of 8 million tons and a coal production of 230 million tons. She was beginning to move forward in the field of machine construction and machine tool building. She was putting up her own steel fabricating plants and building very heavy hydraulic presses.

China's military strength could be matched in Asia only by that of the Soviet Union and the United States. Neither power disposed land forces on the continent sufficient to interdict the application of Chinese power. But each had at its disposal air power, missile power and nuclear weapons sufficient to deter the Chinese.

So far as I could determine, China's military leadership—in contrast to the blustering statements of the Chinese political leaders—was thinking primarily in defensive terms. The military journals and army papers were filled with articles on the danger of U.S. attack, and the military discussions centered on means of countering such an attack.

Should war come, China expected to go it alone. The pact of friendship, aid and alliance which had been signed February 14, 1950, by Stalin and Mao was dead for all practical purposes. This treaty obligated each power to come to the aid of the other in event of attack by Japan or any state allied with Japan—a euphemism for the United States.

But the Chinese did not expect aid from Russia. A number of secret Chinese military papers had fallen into the hands of U.S. intelligence. They contained detailed discussions of Chinese Army tactics and strategy in event of war with the United States. Nowhere was there mention of aid or assistance or intervention by the Soviet Union. All the Chinese plans were based on going it alone.

The Chinese, it was clear from the thinking outlined in these documents, anticipated that war with the United States would be extremely costly. The first move by America would be nuclear bombing of the Chinese nuclear, industrial and political centers. So Peking thought. Chinese tactics were based on long, protracted warfare on land by the survivors of such an initial blow. The Chinese contemplated cellular subdivision of their military forces and the incorporation into paramilitary units of the total population. They anticipated a long, long war. They were certain that in the end, no matter how many millions of Chinese were lost, they would triumph.

Pondering the military data which added up to China's strength and the record of thousands of years of Chinese history, I could not but wonder whether they might not be right.

"The United States is today and now," a Cambodian had told me, "but China is forever."

To the Cambodian, nuclear warfare and its possible consequences were a mystery, but China had been well known for century upon century.

13
The Right to Love

NOTHING ABOUT THE CONTEMPORARY GENERATION OF CHINESE YOUTH
more astounded—and revolted—Russian youngsters than the Chinese
attitude toward love, sex and marriage.

"Imagine!" a young Siberian girl said to me, "they say that Chairman Mao has decreed there shall be no love until they reach the
age of thirty—or twenty-eight for girls. Have you ever heard of
anything like that?"

A Chinese youth delegation recently had made a tour of eastern
Siberia. Many of their opinions were in direct contradiction to those
of their Russian guides. But the most notable contradiction was that
concerning sex. The Russians were astounded to hear the Chinese
say that they were not permitted to have any sexual relations whatever. Indeed, they were not allowed to kiss, to hold hands, to go
out walking together for fear temptation might arise and they would
fall into sin. Dancing was forbidden.

Marriage, the Chinese said, was not to be thought of until they
had completed their education and put in a number of years at
work for the state. Why? Love and relations between the sexes,
they explained, was too distracting. It robbed the state of energies
which should be dedicated to building a new China.

Odd as these views seemed to the Russian youngsters, they
accurately reflected the intensive Chinese campaign for sexual

165

abstinence and late marriage. The Chinese newspapers were filled with exemplary accounts of young women who had delayed their weddings in order to serve the state. Wang Chuan-chuan, twenty-eight years old, was written up in the magazine, *Women of China,* because she had delayed her marriage three times in order not to interfere with her work. Wan Chin-hsui, at twenty-three, had rejected more than ten proposals of marriage because to marry at so early an age would be perfidy to the Communist Party. Tu Chien-hao rejected marriage in favor of dedicating her youthful years to vegetable genetics.

"She began to nurse her fruit of love later than she nursed the good vegetable strains," the Canton *Evening News* wrote. "Her flower of love is now bearing extremely good fruit."

It was not simple puritanism which lay behind the effort to dissuade China's youth from following its natural instincts. The campaign was, in fact, only one aspect of an increasingly desperate effort by the Peking regime to bring under control the torrential fecundity of the Chinese nation.

The government was not depending only upon propaganda, Party discipline and intense external pressures upon the population of child-bearing age. It had put into operation a wide range of control programs. Abortion was encouraged in most parts of the country. It was permitted on the request of the mother without regard to the father's permission. Women who had given birth to three or more children were asked whether they would not undergo an abortion when they appeared at clinics, once again pregnant. Sometimes a mother giving birth to her fourth child was compulsorily sterilized by the attending physician on state order.

After years in which contraceptive devices were hardly obtainable in China they had begun to appear in ample quantities and at cheap prices at sidewalk stalls and cigarette stands.

Sterilization was proposed to fathers of large families.

The campaign for control of births was backed by economic pressures. Ration cards were withheld for children after the third or fourth birth, compelling parents to purchase food on the open market at high prices. Extra cloth rations normally given on the birth of a child were denied after the third birth. Party members were ordered to limit themselves to two children or risk expulsion.

Students were brought under strict regulation. They were not permitted to marry even if of legal age so long as they were enrolled in educational institutions. The state refused to register student marriages. If children were born to students, they were automatically classified as illegitimate and thus not entitled to rations. Paid maternity leaves were refused mothers after the third child.

Among politically conscious students, I was told by visitors to China, Mao's line was meticulously adhered to. But on the population as a whole, so far as I was able to ascertain from talks with travelers, there seemed to have been only modest effect.

For one thing, birth control devices, birth control propaganda and the influence of example and exhortation which strongly affected the Chinese in larger cities had little or no impact in the vast rural areas. Since China's population was still 75 percent nonurban it was obvious that something more would be required to lower China's birth rate materially.

What lay behind the frantic drive to cut down China's rate of population increase?

Only three or four years earlier the Chinese were insisting dogmatically that Malthus was wrong, that there was no such thing as an overpopulation problem, only one of underdistribution. In this they took their lead from pure Marxism. Of the many quarrels which marked Marx' career none was more violent than that with Malthus.

"We are not overpopulated," Party Propagandist Chung Chi-huan typically had said. "On the contrary, we need more people. Ours is a vast country. More laboring heroes are needed to construct a richer and stronger country."

But that kind of propaganda had long since vanished as the

reality of China's population crisis impinged more and more strongly on the consciousness of her leaders.

Not that they were ready frankly to face its enormity even yet. This was to be seen in the frequency with which they continued to cite the ten-year-old estimate of a population of 650 million, projected from the census of 1953. What was the actual population? The very best of the world's demographers were convinced that the Chinese Government simply did not know either the total or the rate of growth. The experts put the total at 750 million to upwards of 800 million in 1966.

At various times Chinese Government spokesmen had said that China's population was growing at a rate of 2.2 percent. At other times they used the figure of 2 percent and sometimes said it ranged between 1.8 and 2.2 percent.

In the summer of 1963 Premier Chou En-lai, speaking to the graduates of Peking University, said that China's birth rate had reached 30 per thousand and must be cut back to 7 per thousand. At that time many Western specialists believed the actual rate was about 40 per thousand. No material reduction had been achieved in the years since 1963.

The variations suggested by these figures was enormous. It ranged from a population increase of more than 10 million a year to one of more than 20 million. Most demographers tended to believe that the annual increase was closer to 20 than 10 million. It was on this calculation that estimates placing China's population in the range of 750 to over 800 million were made.

Even these figures may have been calculated on the low side. A U.S. State Department geographer, Dr. G. Etzel Pearcy, produced estimates in late 1966 which suggested that China's population as of January 1, 1966, may have already reached the level of 760,300,000, 800,292,000 or 894,493,000, depending upon which growth rate was accepted as being correct.

These estimates, like all those concerning China's population, took as a starting point the 1953 Chinese census figure of 576 million for the mainland population. The problem confronting demographers was how to estimate the accuracy of this census. Some specialists calculated it may have understated China's population by a margin as high as 15 percent.

If, as the specialists believed, China's population had increased at least 15 million per year since 1953, her total obviously must be nearing 800 million. Soon China would be adding 100 million to the world's population every four years.

One in every four persons in the world in 1966 was Chinese. If the rate of increase continued without material change, by the mid-1970's her population would easily top one billion. It was increasing at a rate which doubled the total in less than thirty-five years. Each generation China was presenting the world with the equivalent of a new China. Shortly after the start of the twenty-first century China would boast a population of two billion. One of three people in the world would be Chinese.

Nothing like this had occurred since the earth began to assume solid shape. On the day two billion Chinese swarmed across the globe there would be fewer than 300 million Americans, about 350 million Russians and nearly 900 million Indians—insignificant population aggregates beside the titanic totals of China. The world population would then be about seven billion—almost 60 percent in Asia.

These were, to be sure, projections. No demographer could be certain what the graphs of the next thirty years would show. But unless very, very great changes occurred the pattern would not be much different. The world was undergoing a population explosion. Nowhere were the effects more dramatic than in Asia.

The Chinese population was growing with such rapidity that this force, taken alone, seemed quite capable of changing the world balance of power. The enormous pool of manpower would inevitably propel China into the position of No. 1 world power provided her leadership was able to harness this Niagara of humanity.

But as China's population multiplied with Malthusian rapidity her food position went from bad to worse. She had recovered from the most disastrous effects of the introduction of the commune system and some primitive attempts to systematize farm production. Her harvests had been recouped after the floods and droughts of 1963 and 1964. By 1965 she was producing a grain total of close to 179 million metric tons, roughly what she turned out in the best years of the 1950 decade. But in 1965 China had a population which was 75 to 100 million higher than in 1955. To feed this population she had to buy five to six million metric tons of grain abroad. The cost of this grain ranged between $400 and $500 million in hard currency. Herein lay the secret of the existence of Hong Kong. To my surprise I found that China earned by selling to Hong Kong just about the amount of hard currency which she needed to buy grain. Most of this came from selling foodstuffs to Hong Kong. This was only an apparent anomaly. China sold high-cost foods like milk, eggs, fruit, butter, vegetables and meat to Hong Kong. She used the money to buy wheat or rice. She also sold rice and soybeans to Japan. But these exports came from areas which had a surplus of foods. She replaced the exported foods with cheaper grainstuffs purchased with her foreign currency earnings.

Thus far, by delicately balancing sales and purchases, China had made both ends meet. She had gotten by without a famine of the type which had swept the Celestial Kingdom time and time again. She had managed by austere rationing and equitable distribution to maintain the health of her people. There had been suffering and shortages, but nothing to compare with the bad old days. And in late summer, 1966, travelers reported that foodstuffs seemed plentiful in the markets and in the villages. There was every indication of a good crop.

But China's leaders were not lulled by indications that the evil day had been delayed. They knew, even though they might not publicly admit it, that each year there were close to twenty million new mouths to feed, close to twenty million new Chinese to clothe, to house, to shelter.

The future was grim. There was little hope that Chinese agriculture, already strained to the limit, could be expected to boost production at anything like the increase in the population rate. True, the government was making every effort to improve production of chemical fertilizer, to introduce mechanized methods, better seeds, more fruitful irrigation. But even with the best of success this would hardly close the gap.

Foreign purchases already badly strained China's available foreign exchange. Each year the need for grain could be expected to grow. Where would the money come from? And with demands on the available surpluses of Canada, Australia and the United States constantly growing, where would the grain come from even if China raised the money to pay for it?

The dilemma was real and it was acute.

It was this, it seemed plain enough to me, which fired the flames of Chinese aggression, which compelled China's leaders toward a policy of chauvinism, irredentism and adventurism along their frontiers.

I was certain that no strong Chinese government, certainly not the present Communist dictatorship, would willingly let the Chinese people starve. They would take any possible measure to avert the mass famine of the imperial days. They would use every possibility to improve farm production. They would impose the harshest rationing. They would buy as much food as possible, and in an extremity they would even accept relief shipments of grain from the hated United States.

But if all these measures still fell short, would they simply fold their hands and let the forces of nature run their course?

I did not think so. This was contrary to every tenet of activist Chinese Communist philosophy. No. If they did not have enough food for their people or enough land on which to grow it, they would look beyond their borders.

Indeed, I felt certain that they were already looking. How else to explain Chinese insistence upon the return of the vast lands which had been appropriated by the Russian czars? There were those who suggested that these demands were mere propaganda. I did not think so. Especially not after Mao and Khrushchev in their final polemics before Khrushchev's fall in 1964 revealed that the argument over the lost lands was not a recent one. It had been in progress for ten years since the very first trip which Khrushchev and Bulganin made to Peking in the autumn of 1954. At that time Mao put on the table for discussion the question of "rectification of frontiers." Khrushchev angrily refused to discuss it. His anger was understandable. Under the heading of "rectification" Mao had wanted to discuss the return of lands on which millions of Soviet citizens now lived—eastern Siberia, the Maritime areas, much of Soviet Central Asia.

Khrushchev declined to consider the question then, and I had no doubt that Moscow would go on refusing to discuss it. But I did not think Peking would ever take no for an answer. The plain fact was that these lands, particularly those of eastern Siberia and the Maritime Province, were excellent agricultural regions—the last large agricultural regions in the Soviet Union not yet subject to exploitation. The Soviet had plans for the area, but little had been done. This was plainly evident as I traveled through eastern Siberia and the fine farming territory of the Maritimes. I saw mile after mile of beautiful land, unsullied by the plow, whole provinces of virgin lands. One could not travel through the area without understanding how strongly the Chinese must feel to see these millions of acres of fine cultivable land still untouched by human effort—areas where millions of tons of grain and foodstuffs might be raised, where millions of Chinese might be resettled from the crowded and overcultivated areas of the central and northwest regions.

Then there was Mongolia, which, in the Chinese view, presented much the same aspect. It was a country which was hardly populated by Chinese standards—only 1.1 million by latest count. The population was growing slowly, particularly in contrast to Inner Mongolia, which had the highest population growth of any region of China.

So often I had driven over Mongolia's beautiful grass steppes. Now they were used for the most part for the grazing of horses and sheep. Only a comparatively small acreage had been put to the plow and sowed to grain under Soviet exhortation. The Mongols had neither the inclination nor the manpower to cultivate much of their acreage. Yet the crops on the comparatively small acreages which had been sown proved the point which the Chinese were insisting on. The Mongol grasslands could be turned to excellent account if transferred from grazing to plowed usage. Behind the Chinese maneuvers for influence in Mongolia lay a natural desire to acquire these unused lands and settle them with hard-working and productive Chinese farmers, thus assisting in meeting the terrible food problem.

Nor was it only to the north and west that the Chinese looked out on regions which could help to feed their people. When they looked to the south and southwest, when they contemplated the rice surplus areas of Vietnam, of Cambodia, of Thailand, of Burma, they could hardly fail to think how these territories might serve to meet the crisis which overhung them.

It was no accident that a leader like General Ne Win of Burma was concerned over Chinese interest in the routes down from Kunming and the old Burma Road to the rice-rich delta of the Irrawaddy. Burma's rice was China's need. Thailand in recent years had managed to produce an even larger exportable surplus than Burma. Cambodia had more rice than the Cambodians could eat. In normal times Vietnam was a rice exporter.

How long would a hungry China stand by while weak neighbors produced a surplus of the food she needed for survival?

When I looked at the dynamics of China, the chart of her rising population, the ineffectual measures being taken to reduce the birth rate, the relatively ineffective means being taken to increase food production, it seemed to me that one could project on a chart the year when China's rulers would be forced into aggressive action across their frontiers in search of food for the rice bowls of their people.

And that date, I felt certain, must come up within the next decade—possibly sooner if there was a succession of bad crop years.

This was the nightmare of population and food with which Mao and his associates had to live. It was never mentioned in the propaganda. But it was the inner mechanism which gave direction and force to their policies. It had compelled them to abandon the anti-Malthusian theory of Marx and bend every effort to limit their population. It had compelled them to drop pure communes for the sake of attempting to make agriculture more productive. It had forced them to acquire foreign exchange and to trade with hated capitalist countries for food. It was already a dominant—if not *the* dominant—motivation in their economic and foreign policy.

Small wonder that there was in China's posture toward the outer world a constant tone of aggression, of hysteria, of menace. It was fed by the ill-concealed inner contradictions of China's necessities.

So long as China was unable to resolve her problem of food and population, the temptation of Chairman Mao, his associates or his heirs to seek a solution in lands beyond their frontiers each year inexorably grew larger.

Small wonder the Russians had deployed strong forces across the breadth of eastern Siberia and had moved to give Mongolia additional assistance in manning her long borders with China.

But did the hard, cold military line—the line which the Soviet Union and Mongolia pursued on their frontier, the line which underlay the American position in Southeast Asia and which had come to form the basis of India's position—did this barrier of steel and armed power really provide the answer? Was it not like forcing down the lid on a pressure cooker? Would it not insure that when the explosion came it would be more violent, more uncontrollable, more destructive? Did we not already see in the virulence of the Red Guards, in the savage xenophobia of Chinese policy, in the schizophrenic view which Peking held of the outer world, the advance symptoms of precisely such a cataclysm?

So the picture appeared to me from every vantage point from

which I viewed it—be it the Lo Wu Road, the Cambodian jungle trail, the red-earth deserts of Burma, the fog-shrouded Himalayas, the stormy Black Dragon River or the quiet contemplation garden of a Japanese temple.

Typhoon signals were flying over China. Was there any step which we might take, any policy which we might adopt, which gave some hope of averting the onrushing disaster?

14
❦ *War at 200 Meters*

I DO NOT KNOW WHETHER I HAVE BEEN ABLE TO CONVEY THE SENSE of clear and present danger aroused within me by my thirty-thousand-mile journey along China's perimeter. This sense flowed from a simple, clear and repeatedly reinforced impression: China and the United States were far advanced along a course which could lead only to nuclear war.

I do not believe many Americans perceive this possibility with the clarity with which it can be seen from many vantage points in Asia. Not all Asians perceive it. But, chillingly, it is fully recognized in China itself. Indeed, there is good reason to believe that China as far back as early 1965 (when the United States began the build-up in Vietnam) concluded that the American action probably would lead to an attack on China. One can argue the validity of China's assessment. Few Americans, except for a hard-core Pentagon and Air Force group which had long spoiled for an excuse to attack China's nuclear installations, saw the Vietnam action as a prelude to war with China. Regardless of American intent, the Chinese so interpreted it and since that time have based their policy on the likelihood of Sino-American war.

The Chinese expect to fight against the United States alone, without allies, without assistance from the Soviet Union or Communist states allied with Russia. They would not be surprised to see Russia join with the United States. They believe their own propaganda which states that the Kremlin and Wall Street are jointly plotting against China. This is the way the world seems to them. They can see the maneuvers of the United States and the Soviet Union, the efforts by both powers to maintain a line of communications, a path toward *détente* despite the tensions of Vietnam, and they place a paranoid interpretation on these actions.

To most Americans this seems absurd, like a scene out of a play by Ionesco or Kafka. It did not seem absurd to me. I had lived through the last Stalin years in Moscow. I had watched the intensification of paranoia in the Kremlin, the grip of delusion upon the Soviet leadership, the intensity with which Stalin saw enemies everywhere until he really believed that Voroshilov had been a British spy since the days of the Civil War, that agents of the CIA and the British Secret Service had penetrated the Kremlin hospital with the aid of the Jews and were poisoning his associates. Stalin believed these things, and because he did Soviet policy was based upon the formulation that Russia was surrounded by wolves which might attack at any moment. The watchword was vigilance. Enemies were everywhere—beyond the frontiers and within the Soviet borders. Least of all did Stalin trust Communists, especially foreign Communists. He suspected Mao and regarded him not as a genuine Communist but as a man who might be plotting behind his back with God knows whom.

To anyone who had lived in Moscow in the years just before Stalin's death in 1953, who had seen the savage purges sweep the country as Stalin sought, again and again, to rid himself of imaginary enemies and possible plotters; to anyone who had seen the mounting isolation of the Kremlin behind its Iron Curtain; the clamping down on sources of conflicting opinion; the closing of windows through which a clear view of the real world could be obtained, what was happening in China seemed like the rerun of a bad movie.

Stalin's great fear in his last years was that the Soviet Union would be attacked by the United States. The fear in the United States of an attack by Russia was equally vivid. Year by year the conflicting policies of the two powers brought tensions higher and higher: northern Iran in 1946, Greece and Turkey the same year, Berlin in 1948, Korea in 1950. Each side feverishly prepared for war. Russia worked to perfect her nuclear arms. In the Pentagon the hawks talked of "preventive strikes" to smash Russia's nuclear power before it developed.

True, there are differences between the relations of the United States and China in 1967 and those of the United States and Russia in 1949. But there was a resemblance, too. The road to Lo Wu, I found, was not so different from the road to Moscow. The big difference was that in 1949 you could penetrate the Iron Curtain and go to Moscow. You could savor the atmosphere at firsthand, measure the changes, observe the tendencies, experience the fears and frustrations in your own person. Not so with China in 1966. You traveled up to the frontier and looked across. But you got no further.

In Peking it did not seem so strange to consider the Vietnam war as the opening phase of an attack on the China mainland. To Peking it had seemed that in Korea the United States, at MacArthur's insistence, was turning a peninsular conflict into a direct thrust at China. The Chinese felt they had blunted that American thrust and ground it to a dead halt. To Peking the American support of Chiang Kai-shek and Taiwan was part of the same persisting U.S. strategy—an American *place d'armes* close to the China coast, an assault base for attack on the mainland when conditions became propitious. To Peking Taiwan was Chinese soil. They had hoped to capture it, to liquidate the American jumping-off place with the help of Soviet power, backed by the Soviet H-bomb and Soviet ICBM's. They thought they were assured of Soviet support at the time of the Quemoy-Matsu crisis in September, 1958. When the Russians refused to back the proposed Chinese attack, Mao's conviction that Moscow secretly preferred Washington to Peking solidified.

Against this background it was not difficult to see why the attitude of China toward Vietnam essentially differed from that of the Soviet Union. China regarded the conflict as the opening stage of an American attack aimed at her. Russia viewed it, for the most part, as the United States did—as an action which had its origins and objectives strictly within the non-Chinese areas of Southeast Asia. The Russians opposed the American action. They were distressed by it. But they did not see it as a dagger pointed in their direction. In fact, they took sardonic pleasure from the heightening Chinese confrontation with the United States. The Russians were aware of the danger to themselves from a Sino-U.S. war. But, insofar as the United States became more and more engaged in Southeast Asia, insofar as the United States turned from Europe toward the Asian mainland and China, the Russians saw decided advantages. The U.S. posture put great strain on American commitments in Europe and elsewhere. From this Russia stood to gain.

I had heard in the United States much speculation on why Russia and China did not get together over Vietnam. Was it not in their common interest to do so? Granted they were in deep conflict on broader questions, why could they not agree to work together in Vietnam?

It was a good question. For the truth was they were not working well there. They were at cross-purposes. The Russians charged that the Chinese impeded their efforts to send supplies to North Vietnam. Moscow claimed the Chinese would not permit arms and equipment to move by rail across China to Vietnam. The Chinese angrily denied these charges, claiming that the Russians deliberately were concocting incidents to sow propaganda. The truth, said Peking, was that Russia was not supporting Vietnam because there was a "deal" between Moscow and Washington.

In the course of my journey I talked with several persons who had been in and out of North Vietnam and were familiar with what aid was being given by both the Russians and the Chinese. I asked them about the charges and the countercharges.

"It is quite simple," one said. "The Russians insist on sending their supplies by rail across China. The Chinese insist that the supplies go by sea. They say their railroads don't have the capacity to carry the Russian goods. The Russians insist they want to ship by land because the route is quicker and safer."

Are those the real reasons? I asked.

He shrugged his shoulders. Perhaps not, he conceded. It might well be that the Russians wanted to ship by land because then if there were repercussions they would fall on the Chinese. And the Chinese, perhaps, wished the shipments to go by sea because in that event any trouble would concern Russia, not China.

Each country was trying to play the situation so that the other would become involved with the United States. The fact that North Vietnam was not getting the support it needed to keep up the battle against the Americans was of minor consequence to both Russia and China.

Nevertheless, despite her belligerent words, her defiant propaganda, her curt rejection of any step toward easing world tensions, it was apparent when you looked closely at Chinese actions—as I had—that in acts, not words, the Chinese were being careful and cautious. They kept open the one link they had with the United States—the occasional meetings in Warsaw between the U.S. and Chinese ambassadors. They watched patiently as U-2 planes, manned by Nationalist Chinese pilots but serving U.S. purposes, overflew their territory on intelligence missions. They kept the guard up along their sea and southern frontiers but were careful not to provoke actions.

Did this mean, as American policy-makers seemed to think, that China *could not be provoked?* That it was perfectly safe to move up the Vietnamese coast closer and closer to China? To carry out "Inchon" landings behind the lines in the Gulf of Tonkin? To move the war to the Chinese frontier without the danger of another Yalu River?

I did not believe so. Nor, I found, was the American assumption of a continuing placidity and patience on the part of China shared by most Asians. With hardly an exception (the exceptions were mostly Thais, who were, if anything, more belligerent than the most belligerent Americans) the Asians felt certain that there was a definite flash point for China, and that if the United States carried the war more and more strongly farther and farther north, this flash point would be touched off. Indeed, there were a few cynical Asians who insisted that this was what some American commanders counted on, that they hoped to provoke a Chinese reaction so as to give themselves the excuse to do what they had wanted from the start—bomb the Chinese nuclear sites. This estimate of American intentions flowed, for the most part, from Asians who had convinced themselves that China was the prime American objective and that the United States would never have committed such extraordinary forces to Southeast Asia did we not actually intend to attack China.

If my reading of the Chinese situation had validity, it did not seem sensible to assume that China could not be provoked into war. Just the contrary. Behind the façade of her calculated international coolness she was engaged in full-scale preparation for war. This was the reality which somehow escaped the notice of the United States. China expected war and she was making herself ready for war.

The Chinese calculation was that the United States might at any time launch an attack. They were confident that it would be a nuclear attack and that the initial target would be China's nuclear production centers of Lanchow and Paotow; her political capital, Peking; her industrial centers like Shanghai, Tientsin, Mukden, Canton, Hangchow, and all the rest. They expected that within the first hours or days of war American nuclear bombs would fall on all her principal population centers. They anticipated that the death toll would be stupendous—possibly reaching the 300 million figure Mao had suggested.

But, as the Chinese saw it, this was only the opening phase of a war which might go on for decades. And which would end with their victory and the full defeat not only of the United States but of the whole West at the hands of the aroused "backward" peoples of the world.

This, in essence, was what Lin Piao was talking about in his "Long Live the Victory of the People's War."

In that declaration he had argued that the more widespread a war in which the Americans became engaged, the better the chances for defeating them since, once U.S. forces were committed to one area, they had no ability to maneuver in another. This, to his way of thinking, was the virtue of the Vietnam conflict. It tied down so many Americans. China would be an even more spectacular example.

Lin outlined the tactics which China would employ to combat American technological superiority.

"However highly developed modern weapons and technical equipment may be and however complicated the methods of modern warfare," he said, "in the final analysis the outcome of a war will be decided by the sustained fighting of the ground forces, by the fighting at close quarters on battlefields, by the political consciousness of the men, by their courage and spirit of sacrifice."

In other words—*battle at a range of two hundred meters*!

This was the strategy and tactic which China proposed to employ. This was the strategy and tactic in which the People's Liberation Army was being trained.

The United States might drop its nuclear weapons. It might destroy the Chinese cities. It might kill hundreds of millions of Chinese. But it would not defeat China. For after the bombs had fallen an American expeditionary force must come in to seize the land. The Chinese would still be in the field. For they were being trained in small groups, local units in which the whole of the population would participate. They were being trained to hold their fire, not to attack until the enemy came into such close range that his superior technology could not be used. When men were fighting hand to hand or within two hundred meters, modern artillery was of no avail. Airplanes were useless. Nuclear weapons could not be employed.

The viability of the Chinese tactic was being tested, in Lin's view, in Vietnam.

"The United States has made South Vietnam a testing ground for the suppression of people's war" Lin wrote. "It has carried on this experiment for many years and everybody can now see that the U.S. aggressors are unable to find a way of coping with people's war."

The Chinese counted on themselves and themselves alone to defeat the United States once American troops moved onto the mainland in the deadly wake of the nuclear attack. Not that they did not hope for other allies. They were convinced that once the issue was joined in China there would be touched off in Asia, in the Middle East, in Africa and in Latin America new crises, revolts and revolutions which would sap American power and ability to cope with dozens of simultaneous "brushfire" wars. They felt certain that the American attack would mobilize the common peoples of Asia, Africa and Latin America against the United States.

The Chinese calculation could be wrong. Most of the Asians with whom I talked wanted to keep out of war rather than get in. On the other hand, most of the same Asians were convinced that the United States would never win another war in Asia. No white power would. That was their opinion. They did not sympathize with China. Most of them feared China's power and China's aggression. But an American war against China, an American nuclear war? There were not many places in Asia (or the world) where that would win American friends or allies.

Already the stress and strain which had been put upon American policy in Asia by what Asians saw as our single-minded, obsessive preoccupation with Vietnam was fraying the nerves of some of our best friends and most important allies. What would happen in event of escalation into conflict with China? This was what the Asian statesmen feared most. They could see no real limits to such conflict. They had no confidence that it would not spread and undermine or destroy the whole continent.

Would Russia really stay out of such a war? I was confident that Moscow regarded the Sino-Soviet alliance as dead. But to stand by calmly while a whole continent was going up in nuclear flames? I wondered. I wondered very much. No nation except Japan had so vivid perception as the Russians of the reality of nuclear conflict. Russia had suffered so much in World War II, the impressions of death and devastation were still so vivid, that it was not difficult for them to envisage what would happen if nuclear bombs began to rain down. They had sacrificed too much ever to wish for suicidal disaster. But once the nuclear Moloch began to stalk the world, who could tell?

The consequences of American attack on China might not be exactly as Mao Tse-tung or Lin Piao envisaged them. The disaster to China might be far more grave than their limited imaginations conceived. But, on the other hand, the danger to the United States and to the world of total destruction, of being reduced to smoking ruins by remorselessly escalated nuclear conflict, seemed to me to be far, far more real than the American public—and American policy-makers—had any idea.

China was preparing to defend herself in a nuclear war by the only tactics which seemed to her to have a possibility of succeeding. I wondered whether our thinking about that war had really progressed beyond the mushroom cloud of the first big bang.

Of course, events did not have to take so fatal a course.

In all truth, the impression in most parts of Asia was that the United States was moving ahead toward a military solution in Vietnam. There were few Asians who doubted the ability of the massive American military machine to bring the Vietnamese to their knees. After all, said the Asians, you are fighting one of the smallest, weakest countries in Asia. There shouldn't be any question as to who will win, now that you are bringing your force to bear.

Nor was this all. The general impression in Asia was that the forces of Communism were on the run. They cited the downfall of Sukarno in Indonesia and the terrible toll taken there of the Communist Party and its supporters. They cited the disintegration of the Communist movement in many countries as a result of the split between Moscow and Peking. They cited the enormous setback to Chinese influence which had followed the emergence of the Red Guards and the radical new line in Peking. They cited China's defeats in Africa and elsewhere, the downfall of Nkrumah, the weakening of Chinese influence as a result of the confrontation with India.

Everywhere, or so it seemed to the Asians, the high tide of Communism and of Chinese influence was receding. No longer did it seem likely that, as Peking had proclaimed, the East Wind would prevail over the West Wind. Instead, the signs favored the West Wind.

The West Wind would prevail if—if Vietnam was not permitted to escalate into full-scale conflict with the Chinese; if Asia was spared open confrontation between the United States and China; if the American commanders did not overreach themselves and touch off the Chinese explosion.

There was another danger which many Asians saw. This was the danger that with American preoccupation with military power, with the dropping of ever heavier loads of bombs, the imposing of ever heavier fire power on Vietnam, the political ends of the conflict would be lost sight of. That, in fact, the United States would think once it had burned, bombed and blasted the Viet foe out of existence the job in Asia had been done.

This to the Asians would be a fatal error. For it was when the bombs stopped falling that the real task began. And of American ability to carry this out they had substantial doubt. Unless the United States was prepared to maintain eternally an enormous garrison in Southeast Asia the only long-term guarantee of stability lay in creating a new political structure in Vietnam impervious to Communist subversion or assault. There was no one in Asia—myself included—who could see that the United States had taken effective steps toward erecting a strong, politically stable government in

Vietnam. Indeed, I felt that when the fighting ended on the battle-field the shaky pseudo government of South Vietnam would simply collapse. Again and again I was told: "The smartest thing the Viet-cong can do is to give up. The moment the fighting stops they have won the war."

There seemed to me to be no sign that the United States per-ceived this danger. Nor that we perceived the erosion of the American position caused by the ever-rising bomb levels in Viet-nam. For the more troops we put in, the more money we poured in (and it was going in at the rate of $2 to $3 billion a month by 1967), the less heed we paid to the rest of Asia. There was no money left to provide for the pressing problems of a dozen Asian coun-tries. Nor was there time or manpower available in Washington to concentrate on questions like India's food, Burma's economy, the Soviet wooing of Afghanistan, or Japan's hesitant steps toward international political independence. These matters did not get the attention of the Secretary of State or the White House. The President's desk was stacked with urgent military matters con-cerning Vietnam. There was little room for anything else.

The results were appalling. It was not only the note sounded again and again by the Russians that something *must* be done if Vietnam was not to send down the drain all vestiges of *détente*. It was not merely that India and Japan hung on the brink of entering the nuclear arms race because the United States and Russia, split over Vietnam, were unable to reach an easily negotiable com-promise on nonproliferation of nuclear weapons.

All of this was tragic. Even more tragic was the devastation in Europe—the ruin of NATO; the alienation of France; the grudging, almost niggardly, support now evoked of American policies by our best friends, Britain and Germany; the rapid movement of the Soviet Union to strengthen diplomatic and economic ties with France, Italy, the Low Countries and Scandinavia.

The truth was that the American position in Europe, which had been our Gibraltar since the end of World War II, had been so badly shaken that it was dubious it could ever be restored.

The United States had assumed that in due course it would be able to patch things up. Perhaps. But each day, each month, each year that passed made the task more difficult.

And what of the Soviet Union? The American calculation was that Russia and China had split so far apart that they could never get together again. It was this which gave the American generals a feeling of security in maneuvering against China. They could talk freely of nuclear pre-emptive strikes against Chinese nuclear facilities because they did not believe such action would evoke a counter-nuclear strike by Russia.

Could they be sure?

No.

All I needed was a quick look at history to understand that no policy based on the assumption of a permanent split between Russia and China was built on a secure foundation.

The truth was that relations between Soviet Russia under Stalin and Communist China under Mao had been secretly hostile. I had long been convinced that Stalin had plotted to undermine Mao, that he had touched off the Korean War with that thought in mind and that he had secret allies within Mao's inner circle. But when Stalin died the first act of his successors was to attempt a *rapprochement* with China. They had succeeded in considerable measure. From 1954 through 1959 China and Russia worked fairly well together.

Or take another example. Before Stalin died it was a cliché to insist that Moscow policy would not change when the Old Dictator died. Why? Because he had surrounded himself with men who believed just as he did. They would inevitably carry forward precisely the same policies. The same thing was now said of China, of Mao and his associates.

Nothing could be more unsound. George Kennan, during his brief term as U.S. Ambassador to Moscow in the summer of 1952, correctly forecast that Stalin's successors inevitably and inexorably would be *compelled* to change his policies, to try to achieve a *détente* with the United States. Stalin's associates, he said, were intelligent, able men. They could see that Stalin's policies had failed, that they had brought the country to the brink of disaster. Their hands were tied so long as Stalin lived. But the moment he died they moved precisely as Kennan forecast—toward a *détente* with the United States. Why would not history repeat itself in China?

There was another notable example to bear in mind. In the years leading up to World War II there were many confrontations in the world, but none more basic than that between Hitler's Germany and Stalin's Russia. These two were the logical, the classic enemies. In estimates of the world situation statesmen started with the formula that whatever else might change Russia and Germany would remain implacable foes. It was this conviction which led Neville Chamberlain to engage in such dilatory talks with Moscow in 1939 looking to an alliance against Hitler. He firmly believed Stalin had no other place to turn. He was wrong. Stalin turned to Hitler and the "impossible" happened—the alliance of Nazism and Communism.

Once the Nazi-Soviet pact was made, it was assumed that this, too, was an immutable fact. That it would go on and on forever.

But, of course, it did not. Hitler attacked Stalin and history took quite a different turn.

Who would have the temerity to say in the light of these so recent historical examples that a similar dramatic turn could not occur in Soviet-Chinese relations? Should Mao die, would not his successors act as statesmen and prudent men and repair the rifts rent in the Communist world, enlist once again the protection of Russia's nuclear shield? And even without Mao's death could not a secret, sudden move end the split in the Communist camp? Was not this in Moscow's mind when it dropped hints in 1966 that it might be confronted with a request to intervene in China on behalf of one faction or another of a divided Chinese Party?

I thought it could be. I did not think, to be honest, that the Soviet-Chinese rift could long stay mended. It seemed clear to me that historic and balance-of-power factors would soon drive Russia and China apart again. But that did not preclude their working together for a period of some years, particularly if driven toward each other by the centripetal pressure of U.S. military power.

What then? Might not the United States, thinking that it confronted only a backward China, a tyro in nuclear armament, find itself suddenly facing its equal in the terrible means of making death by smashing matter?

So far American policy in Southeast Asia had been based on the theory of escalation upon escalation. The only logical end to such a process was escalation to the nuclear stage.

Mao was prepared for that whether Russia came reluctantly to his side or not. His tactics, expounded by Lin Piao, accepted nuclear war. China would not collapse under the atom bomb. The Chinese were certain of that. It seemed to me that they had reason for their confidence. To the outside world the events of 1966, the rise of the Red Guard movement, the mystical reliance upon the "thought of Chairman Mao," seemed to be a latter-day manifestation of the same nationalist chauvinism which sent the fanatical Boxers into the streets of Peking at the turn of the century.

To be sure, the movement had many of the same aspects. But it had another. It was, if we read the open statements of the Chinese leaders, a preparation of the country for war. The young people of China were being steeled for sacrifice, hardship, bloodshed and death by the experience of going into the streets, standing shoulder to shoulder, fighting shoulder to shoulder. The nation as a whole was being tempered. Stalin had purged his General Staff, had shot thousands of top Party leaders in the years just before World War II. His self-inflicted blows had weakened Russia. But they had, in a sense, unified the country as well. It seemed clear to me that Mao with his Red Guards was putting China through a toughening-up process. He was giving it a dress rehearsal for war, for the grimmest experience it would ever have to face.

A friend of mine emerged from China in the autumn of 1966, a person who had known China long before the rise of Mao and who had intimately followed the fateful progression of events of recent years in Peking.

"China expects the United States to attack," he said. "She is certain of it. The Red Guards have been created to mobilize the country—and its youth—for war. It is coming and the Red Guards will be ready. Just watch. Soon they will begin to concentrate more and more on military matters."

This observer readily granted that there had been excesses by the Red Guards, that they had encountered resistance, that they had attacked institutions and individuals perfectly loyal to the regime.

"But they have rooted out every secret source of opposition," he said. "They are like an angry wind. They blow down some good trees, but they destroy everything rotten, old, weak."

The A-bombs and the H-bombs might rain down. But Mao intended that within the ruins of a poisoned land Chinese fighting cells would remain. The Americans would have to enter this deadly desert, seeking out the caves, the hovels, the hamlets, the endless wastes, the mountainsides, the deserted nooks, the underground refuges, and fight it out man to man. Not with just a few Chinese—for even, as Mao had said, if 300 million died, 300 million would survive. Since 1957, when he had made that statement, more millions had come into being. Even if 300 million were killed by the Americans (and I did not know of an American who could face that possibility or that figure without flinching), there would remain possibly 400 and more likely 500 million Chinese, ready and waiting, with bayonet, dagger, hand grenade and Molotov cocktail—for combat within two hundred meters.

Was there any means by which the United States might shift the tide, change the odds on nuclear war, avert the holocaust which so plainly was advancing?

It seemed to me that there was. The time was late, the task was difficult, but it was not beyond American capabilities.

To succeed, the approach must be to the fundamentals. If, as I felt, the key to the China problem was food and population, then the approach must be toward a solution of this dilemma. China must be guaranteed food and technical resources—a World Food Pool— to meet her needs and avert the danger of famine. She herself was seeking to bring her population under control. She must have the best of technical assistance for this task.

I realized that even if agreement on this goal could be achieved it would not be easy to approach China or to win her acceptance although the program would be to her advantage. In the paranoid state of her leadership any approach would be branded a trick and a device, and any proposal would be seen as an aggressive scheme.

The first step would be to win some measure of her confidence. The United States had little prospect of achieving this. The Soviet Union could hardly help. Neither could India. There were only three powers with a chance of success—Japan, Canada, and France. The first approach must be made through them.

But that was not likely to succeed so long as the Vietnam conflict was in a state of constant escalation. There must be a standstill there, some approach toward a settlement, some step which would be clearly and distinctly recognized as a genuine move toward stabilization and peace. Vietnam had paralyzed both the neutrals and our friends. There was nothing they could do to begin to bring the tensions down to bearable levels.

The first steps would be the most difficult ones because of the critical nature of the Chinese psychosis. And there would be almost equally difficult steps to follow.

Only the United States could take those steps. They must be steps which unmistakably demonstrated our desire not for victory in Vietnam but for a solution which would place the fate and future of Southeast Asia neither in American nor in Chinese hands. We must proclaim our determination for an Asian solution and make it stick. The solution then must be advanced by Asians, negotiated by Asians, guaranteed by Asians, backed by Asians. The Asian backing must be as wide as Asia was wide. Not just a solution advanced by Asian states allied with or sympathetic to the United States. Not a solution backed by Asian states sympathetic to China or hostile to the United States. It must be an all-Asian solution in which India, Japan, Burma, Thailand, Indonesia, the Philippines, all the states participated. The Asians themselves must set up a stable regime in Southeast Asia and tell the United States and China, in effect: "Stay out!"

We must devise and carry out a calculated program to end China's dangerous isolation, to correct the incredible distortion in the lens with which she viewed the outer world.

For a decade argument had raged as to whether China should be admitted to the United Nations. There was no longer room for argument. China must be dragged, kicking and screaming, into the United Nations assembly. This would not be easy. Not because of a difficulty of getting the votes. China's admission could be attained the moment the United States let it be known she favored such a course. The favorable vote could be counted upon. But not Chinese acceptance of the invitation. In the years in which the Chinese had built their wall of isolation higher and higher they had created a whole dossier of conditions which must be satisfied before she would join the UN. Basically, the Chinese were insisting on a radical revision of the UN charter, one which would take the power away from the United States, Russia and the West and vest it in the nations with the big populations—China and Asia. There were many other demands, most of which could not possibly be met.

Yet somehow China must be brought into the community of nations. She must be placed in a position where she would be exposed to daily contact with reality. She must face the pros and cons of normal diplomatic intercourse, be compelled to open her eyes to the distinctions between Moscow and Washington and between what she called Revisionism and Capitalism.

There was nothing more dangerous to the world than the rise of the enormous Chinese state, barricaded behind walls which gave her only the most limited knowledge of what went on beyond her borders, cut off from ordinary personal contact, literary interchange, philosophical dialogue and commercial trade—all the media which enabled peoples to understand societies alien to their own. If China had been a tiny state in the Himalayas, her lack of integration into the world would have made little difference. But she was the greatest nation in the world in terms of population. She was on the way to becoming the most powerful society which the world had ever seen.

There was no more urgent task on the agenda of humanity than the creation of a framework of relationships which would enable China to live in peace with us and vice versa.

The United States had had no diplomatic relations with Communist China since Mao proclaimed his state October 1, 1949. The rise of a chauvinistic, xenophobic, bitterly anti-American China could be blamed in no small part to utter lack of contact between America and China in nearly two decades. But it did not seem to me desirable to attempt as a first or even as an early step to establish diplomatic relations between Peking and Washington. The Chinese had made clear that they would reject any bid for recognition unless a series of prior conditions were agreed to.

I did not think we could or should agree to most of these conditions. But it seemed high time that we begin discussing the issue of recognition with the Chinese, even if it merely led to seemingly protracted talks.

We needed more than almost anything closer and more intimate contacts with China. We needed to know more—much more—about this country which might be our most dangerous enemy but which might also be turned into a valuable associate. It was too easy, I thought, to forget that in the past America and China had been warm friends. It was too easy to assume that because China was now an intractable opponent she could not become a friend and even an ally. If we looked at history, we could see that it was littered with instances in which erstwhile enemy countries had become friends. To take our own recent past as an example: we had fought bitter wars with Germany and Japan. Yet today we numbered both among our closest friends. Could this happen with China? Why not?

China faced a century of incredible tasks. The most urgent were those of food and population. Beyond them lay industrial and social development, economic organization, education, scientific revolution. There was no nation and no people with so great a pool of skills and genius as China. The United States possessed the technical and scientific know-how which could shorten her long road upward from feudalism to the technological age. There was no reason, once political tensions were eased, why the United States should not enter into partnership with China for the long pull ahead. This thought might seem utopian when read against the invective spewed forth from Peking. It might seem anathema when placed in juxtaposition with American antipathy to Chinese Communism and its evils. To be sure, it would make strange reading in Peking, where America was portrayed as Monster-land, waiting to smash China to smithereens.

And it was just possible that one hidden factor might be working, however faintly, in Peking toward a *rapprochement* with the United States. Certainly, Mao thought war with the United States was more likely than not. Certainly, he felt that the United States represented the great immediate threat. But the No. 1 enemy in the view of the Chinese Party was actually Soviet Russia. Here there was a hatred and emotion which surpassed any Chinese feeling toward the United States. It was akin to that of a lover betrayed, of a soldier against a traitor or to an act of desertion in time of dire need. America, in a sense, was the capitalist enemy to be expected and anticipated in a world governed by the rulebook of Marx. But Russia—Communist Russia—was the unfaithful ally, the renegade friend.

The hard task would be to take the first step—and make it stick. Once the progression of history had been turned in a new direction, we—and China—might be stunned by the rapidity with which an entirely different relationship emerged.

It would be difficult. But the alternative was disaster—the possibility of world nuclear suicide. Almost any difficulty was worth attempting to save the world from such a fate.

More than seventy years ago Lafcadio Hearn wrote a brief essay on the future of the Far East.

He said that the central question was one of food and population for, as he quoted Lord Tennyson: "When all men starve, the wild mob's million feet will kick you from your place."

The struggle for food and the increase of population, he predicted, would eventually pit West against East:

The World can support only a certain number of millions, perhaps between two and three thousand millions. The struggle must go on. And as its intensity increases, the struggle must be a struggle for the possession of the Whole World. Then the weaker races must give way. How give way? Disappear from the face of the Earth. Which will give way— Far West or Far East?

The Far East, he concluded, would win the struggle—win it with the weapons of the West, win it by adopting the aggressive tactics of the West. China, he thought, was the great danger. Because of her intelligence, her natural ability, her enormous size. She was too vast to conquer, too solid to disintegrate, too skilled a rival of the West.

If the Chinese had not been dangerous before, it was simply because they had stayed at home. . . . Fortunately for the West, China moves slowly. She has not yet adopted to any extent the industrial methods and the machinery of Western countries. She is only preparing herself for war. . . . The Chinese can call out 1,200,000 soldiers already; and when these shall have all been armed and disciplined like western troops, no power dare attack China.

But it is quite certain that China will eventually also adopt Western sciences and industries. That will be the greatest danger. For it is not by war that the future of races will be decided. It is by industrial and scientific competition.

Hearn's words could have been written yesterday. The dangers which he foresaw have come to pass. The world stands on the verge of a war of races, utilizing technologies and tactics of which Hearn did not dream.

Yet, or so it seemed to me, there was still a chance that ingenuity and intelligence might spare us the catastrophe. The road to Lo Wu led to as dangerous a cul-de-sac as I had ever encountered. The prospects for emerging might not be bright. But the possibilities did exist. There were those in Moscow and in Washington who on March 4, 1953, saw nothing but nuclear disaster ahead. On March 5, 1953, Stalin died and the tide turned.

It could happen in China as well. The only thing which would make catastrophe inescapable was a conviction that it could not be averted. So long as we did not accept it as inevitable it need not be so.

The first steps would be the most difficult. Many Americans would think them politically impossible. Yet the choice was clear. We must act or face possible obliteration. Better the political courage to take tough decisions which would save the nation and our way of life than the hesitation or hypocrisy which would doom us to disaster.

Index

ABOUT THE AUTHOR

Veteran reporter Harrison E. Salisbury began his newspaper career while still in college. While attending the University of Minnesota, he worked nights as a reporter and rewrite man for the United Press in St. Paul, and edited the college paper as well. After graduation, he started on the old Minneapolis *Journal* as a $15-a-week cub reporter. Subsequently (in 1930) he joined the United Press, where he covered stories in Chicago, Washington, and New York. In 1943 he was made London manager and director of European coverage for the U.P. He became head of the Moscow Bureau in 1944, spending eight months there.

He was later U.P. Foreign Editor. In 1949 Mr. Salisbury joined the *New York Times*. From 1949 to 1954 he was Moscow correspondent for the *Times*. Upon his return to the United States Mr. Salisbury wrote a series on his observations in Russia which won for him the 1955 Pulitzer Prize.

Since his Moscow assignment he has revisited Russia on three occasions, traveling extensively throughout the U.S.S.R., including Siberia and Outer Mongolia. He reads and speaks the Russian language and is presently working on a book on the siege of Leningrad. He is now an assistant managing editor of the *Times*.

Format by Katharine Sitterly
Set in Linotype Caledonia
Composed, printed and bound by The Haddon Craftsmen, Inc.
HARPER & ROW, PUBLISHERS, INCORPORATED

301.2951
S167o

14163

SALISBURY

Orbit of China

ST. PHILIP'S COLLEGE
Not to be taken from the Library
without permission